FIND OUT WHY ADOLESCENT RAGE
CAN SPIN OUT OF CONTROL . . .
WHY THE THRILL TO KILL LURES KIDS TO MURDER.

WATCH FOR THE WARNING SIGNS
THAT CAN STOP A TRAGEDY:

- Abruptly abandoning old friends for new ones
- An unwillingness to allow parents to meet new friends
- A drop in grades at school or abandonment of interest in school
- Rapid change in moods or unusually severe mood swings
- Increasing defiance of regulations
- Increasing conflict with authority figures
- Increasing secretiveness
- Profound laziness or lack of interest in normal activities
- Withdrawal from family gatherings and activities
- Abrupt and negative changes in physical appearance or hygiene
- Avoidance of home, especially by persistently staying out late at night
- Money, alcohol, or prescription drugs missing from home

WHEN GOOD KIDS
KILL

MICHAEL D. KELLEHER

A DELL BOOK

Published by
Dell Publishing
a division of
Random House, Inc.
1540 Broadway
New York, New York 10036

Dell books may be purchased for business or promotional use or for special
sales. For information please write to: Special Markets Department, Random
House, Inc., 1540 Broadway, New York, N.Y. 10036.

Dell® is a registered trademark of Random House, Inc., and the colophon is a
trademark of Random House, Inc.

ISBN: 0-440-23622-3

Reprinted by arrangement with Praeger Publishers

Printed in the United States of America

Published simultaneously in Canada

January 2000

10 9 8 7 6 5 4 3 2 1

OPM

For the children—all of them.

CONTENTS

ACKNOWLEDGMENTS

Throughout the several books I have written, I have never worked alone. I believe this is true for all writers, regardless of their area of specialization. Researching and writing this book was a unique experience for me, because the subject touched me in such a deeply personal way. For this incredible adventure I am indebted to several special individuals who helped me enormously along the way.

I am deeply grateful to Catherine Lyons, who originally suggested the idea for this book. She has worked with me on four previous books, always providing advice that was timely, relevant, and sensitive. It was her belief that I could do a good job with this tough subject. I hope she is not disappointed with the results.

My longtime friend Brian Sobel has been a source of encouragement and optimism throughout the writing of this book and others. He has never failed to provide guidance, support, and direction when I needed it most. I truly value his sage advice. More importantly, Brian is the father of a wonderful and successful teenager—precisely the audience I hope to reach in this book.

All my work relies on the love and friendship of my life partner, Cindy L. Kelleher. She has proven tireless and enduring throughout, always ready to hear the most outrageous specu- lation and persistent in her ability to keep me motivated and focused. It is for her, as well as myself, that I strive. However, her most important and appreciated role has always been as the mother of our children, who are my most valued friends.

Like countless other parents, I owe much of what I have learned of living and loving to my children—Kerry, Katie, Mi- chael, and Jeff. Each of them has passed through their teenage years successfully, and each has made me immensely proud. They have my abiding love and gratitude for giving me a funda- mental perspective of the rigors and wonders of adolescence, along with their unique, invaluable companionship as adults. I truly hope this book is worthy of the important, often unspo- ken, lessons I have learned from each of them.

INTRODUCTION

Consider this classic American credo: "There are good kids, and there are bad kids." Most of us first heard this phrase as children, and we have come to know it well in our adult lives. Many of us have used it in casual conversation, sometimes offering it as a troubled and uncertain explanation for the often-inexplicable actions of our children, our neighbor's children, or society's children. The majority of Americans accept this concept of "good kids and bad kids" as a simple truism—a statement of belief that requires little thought, because it seems to accurately reflect the condition of our contemporary society as well as the intimate experiences of our own lives. However, at best, this belief is a dangerous oversimplification, one that is frequently used to distance ourselves from a complex and growing national problem. At worst, it is an unconscious act of surrender to potential violence, a thinly veiled condemnation of our own children and, therefore, our own future.

According to this popular and contemporary notion, bad kids are easily identified, often feared, and irretrievably destined for failure—or worse. Perhaps as teenagers they have aligned themselves with a recognized, highly organized, and feared gang; alternatively, they may have formed a loose association with small, localized groups comprised of similar and (to many adults) questionable individuals. Often they flaunt their presence with peculiar dress, distinguishing speech patterns, or preferences in music and entertainment that seem foreign, unsavory, and unsettling to their parents and other adults.

These kids delight in giving the impression that they do not value the traditional sanctions and expectations of an older, allegedly wiser society. They often view conformity as a sign of weakness, unless that conformity is indicative of loyalty to their peers. These teenagers may be unwilling to interact with their parents or other adults in an open way, even when it is to their advantage to do so. Their vision of the future may not be as clear as it could be, and they may even work vigorously at distancing themselves from the unresponsive and more established society that surrounds them. Sometimes they push their activities beyond the structure of the law, testing the limits of what is acceptable, avoidable, or tolerable. At times they may act well apart from the accepted norms of our society, with varying degrees of success and punishment as an inevitable result.

If, by the common definition of the term, such teenagers are thought to be "bad kids," then they *must* do bad things, even though the essential meaning of "bad" varies wildly among those who judge their actions. In their teenage years some youth may begin to show a sudden disinterest in school, a disregard for traditional and expected responsibilities, a withdrawal from emotional bonding with their parents, and an obvious disdain for the values of any generation but their own. A few will become extremely withdrawn, secretive, argumentative, and aggressive or violent. However, whatever disturbing form these critical years of abrupt change may take, we as a society stubbornly claim to know instinctively when our children begin to do bad things, even though we are often at a loss to define the concept with any precision. When our children engage in undesirable activities or behavior we become concerned, fearful, defensive, frustrated, and sometimes angry. We may consider these unexpected actions by our children as dire warning signs—the fearful, unsettling markers along the path to adulthood by which we decide when a particular child is, at his or her root, a bad kid.

Sadly, some of these adolescents *do* eventually earn the unshakable definition of "bad," by their overt acts of mayhem and violence. Some of the crimes of these teenagers are so horrific that their impact seems to leave no room to consider any question of goodness. By our own definition, such teenagers *must* be inherently bad, simply because their crimes are so heinous. The media is replete with examples of kids who have committed aggressive and reprehensible crimes after a long history of flagrantly violating the law. Their young lives are abruptly shattered in a final explosion of ultimate violence against family, friends, rivals, or society—and their victims are many.

It is common to learn that these teenage criminals typically arose from a childhood saturated with poverty, neglect, abuse, and an uncaring, indifferent family environment. Such disturbing stories are legend in America and common fare for the press. The awful crimes of these teenagers are known to most of us, and their impact tends to make us fear all youth more than we should. In the end, because of our concerns for our own children and ourselves, we struggle even harder to recognize the genuine warning signs of impending disaster—to be secure in our absolute knowledge of "good kids" and "bad kids." Unfortunately, it seems that we are tilting at windmills.

The irony of this understandable reaction to a society plagued with violent youth is that we fail to comprehend the complexities of the real issues. Instead, we see only the two options of good and bad. As a result, we strive to keep firmly, and often blindly, to our prosaic definitions of "good kids" and "bad kids." Because of our own uncertainty, we can often be quick to condemn without understanding, too ready to fear without knowledge, and too often prepared to support our very personal definitions of "good kids" and "bad kids" simply because they are familiar and comfortable. Given the complexity and dangers of American society, this kind of reaction is very human; however, it has led to a belief system about our children that is far too simplistic and perhaps even dangerous.

When we read of a good kid who has committed a vicious, gruesome crime, we are ready to look for some subtle, covert motivation that will not destroy our basic credo but rather explain the inexplicable. After all, there are good kids and bad kids—or so we *must* believe. If a teenager who has always been viewed as honorable, trustworthy, compliant, and conscientious suddenly commits a violent, explosive crime, the prosaic explanation is that he or she was in reality *not* a good kid. As sudden as his or her crime proved to be, we instantly set to work to reorganize our definition of the goodness and badness of youth so that our basic credo will remain alive and well. In this way, we can for a time set aside our fears and once again wrap ourselves in the warming, comforting definitions of good and bad that we have come to value so highly.

The reality that is presented to us by kids who lash out in acts of unexpected, horrible violence threatens to destroy our personal definitions of good and bad. The actions of these teenagers are clear and devastating, even though their motivations seem foreign, frightening, and frequently beyond understanding. Their crimes also threaten to forever annihilate our basic beliefs about all children—our own children as well as others. What these teenagers do when they lash out in violence tends to throw into question the very foundations upon which we try to build an understanding of all youth. Yet if we are to ever come to a genuine knowledge of why our children commit such brutal crimes, particularly kids who have demonstrated no inclination for violence, we cannot hold fast to a credo that seeks to make them definable by two amorphous and changing qualities, "good" and "bad." If we are willing to put aside our natural, instinctive fears and work to understand these adolescents as we would hope to be understood *by* them, we must first come to the realization that our long-cherished belief in good kids and bad kids is outdated, oversimplified, and fundamentally wrong.

In truth, good kids sometimes act very badly, and bad kids often act with honor and truthfulness. As a society, we can and should recognize both good and bad actions. We *should* strive to reward those members of our society who contribute in a positive way, while we work toward eliminating those actions that threaten our peace, our culture, and our lives. However, it is a mistake to blindly and universally identify the actor with his or her actions. They are not the same things, even though it is sometimes reassuring to believe that they are.

When violence strikes at our family, our nation, or us, there are reasons waiting to be understood and motivations crying out to be discovered. Without an effort to move beyond the mere punishment of an individual or group who has violated our societal norms, we run the risk of never coming to an understanding of why violence so plagues our nation. Worse, we overlook opportunities to create a better, safer society for our children and ourselves.

From time to time, we read a horrifying story about a good kid who has gone disastrously wrong. Perhaps it is an honor student, loving son, and promising athlete who suddenly and brutally murders his mother in an inexplicable rage over a minor family issue. It may be a teenage mother who kills and discards her newborn baby after hiding her pregnancy from her parents and friends. There are many possibilities, even though these types of crime are relatively rare in our society. In the media and on television these adolescents are generally portrayed as inherently good individuals who have somehow gone horribly astray. Their stories are sensationalized in the press and are often accompanied by wild, exaggerated, and unfounded conclusions. The angles of the stories that surround these teenagers frequently dwell on the obvious disparity between the positive, loving, traditional background of the perpetrator and the single moment of horror that redefined the entire meaning of his or her young life. These are the most

troubling cases—the brutal incidents of unconscionable violence that threaten to overturn all we believe about our children and ultimately ourselves. However, the stories of these
crimes and their perpetrators are not simple. There are no
easy, straightforward questions of "good" and "bad" in most
of these tragedies.

When good kids kill, there is a reason—somewhere. When
they murder, even though the act is blatantly horrible and
wrong, it is irrational to believe that the crime sprang fully
formed from some ill-defined, vacuous, and insensitive soul.
That is rarely, if ever, the truth. When a teenager lashes out
in extreme violence, we must look beyond his or her crimes,
regardless of their horror, and search out the reasons *why*
the crime occurred. In many cases we can do this, if we are
willing to face the issues honestly and move beyond the temptation to quickly categorize either the perpetrators or the victims. In some cases, however, it seems impossible to understand
the violence that has occurred. In some instances, we just do
not know enough—yet.

If we truly care to understand why those children we once
categorized as good became so bad, so quickly, we have no
choice but to set aside our simple assessment of these individuals and squarely face the complex forces that impelled
them to violence. To do anything less is to abrogate our responsibilities as members of a forward-looking society and
forever surrender our hope for a less violent future.

1

INCONCEIVABLE CRIMES

Crime hides, and by far the most terrifying things are those which elude us.

Georges Bataille
The Trial of Gilles de Rais

America is a frighteningly violent nation, at least in terms of the number of citizens who are the victims of violent crimes each year. Few of us would like to admit this fact openly, and most of us—especially those of us who are parents—do what we can to avoid physical aggression and violence against our children or ourselves. However, despite our best intentions we persistently surround ourselves with the icons of aggression, and often unconsciously, we enthrone violence in subtle and countless ways in our daily lives. This is particularly true if one is an average American male.

Certainly, if we are a typical male, we regularly listen to news reports, watch a great deal of television each day, and try to read for pleasure or information whenever we find the time in our busy schedules. When we undertake these routine, pleasurable, daily activities, our senses are inevitably drawn to the dark and violent side of our national experience. When we seek out one of the countless forms of entertainment available in our communities, we find that much of it is based on themes of aggression, hostility, and confrontation. In fact, these themes of aggression and violence are unavoidable in American society.

Even in our play we are frequently aggressive and confrontational. Most of us are deeply interested in one or more professional sports, and we typically pride ourselves in the accomplishments and victories of our teams—sometimes, at any cost. For many of us such aggressive and violent competitions as football, hockey, or professional boxing have become a staple in our entertainment diet. In them, the physical assault of one player against another is an accepted, even anticipated, element—if it is not the entire point of the event itself.

As a typical American male (usually beginning in adolescence), we are made keenly aware of our competitive, indefatigable, "don't tread on me" national spirit, which we try to nurture and emulate in every aspect of our lives. This classic American attitude and inviolable self-perspective carries enormous historical importance and bequeaths a deep sense of tradition to most of our citizens. Even as we grow older and more cautious in navigating the unpredictable, sometimes dangerous, byways of life, we may still display this aggressive and dangerous sense of competitiveness with unconscious regularity. One of the most obvious examples of this can be found in every large American city: the endless parade of otherwise genteel, conservative men who commute to and from work in their own automobiles each day, many exhibiting overt, senseless aggression behind the wheel. Certainly, if we are young and less sensitive to the inevitability of our own death, we are even more apt to take risks and give little thought to the meaning and impact of our aggressive behavior.

In any case and at any age, we unconsciously saturate our lives with the elements and icons of aggression and violence, because that is our national tradition and culture. This is not to say that we are an evil, mean-spirited people, who undervalue life—far from it. In fact, during times of crises at the local, national, and even international level, Americans have traditionally and persistently given generously of themselves, regardless of their individual relationships with those in peril. However, despite this sensitivity to others, we remain a violent nation at our core—one of the most violent on this planet. It is our tradition and our culture. Sadly, violence is also the legacy we pass on to our children.

In this country we count the citizens who are murdered each year by their countrymen in the tens of thousands. In fact, we really cannot say with precision how many of our citizens are killed each year in this way. We know that in recent years the annual number is at least twenty thousand, and possibly closer to thirty thousand. Regardless of the statistics we employ, it is clear that the crime of murder in America is a national epidemic. We have all learned that we are not safe from violence in this country, and our fears for the well-being of our children and ourselves are not unreasonable.

We have also learned much about the kind of American who commits murder. For example, we know that the typical murderer is a male, over the age of eighteen, who probably

Figure 1.1
Age of Known Murder Offenders in the U.S.

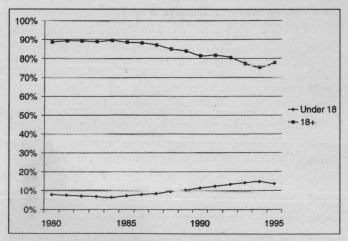

Source: Howard N. Snyder and Terrence A. Finnegan, *Easy Access to the FBI's Supplementary Homicide Reports. 1980–1995* (Washington, DC: Office of Juvenile Justice and Delinquency Prevention, 1997).

had some form of relationship with his victim. We also know that American women rarely commit murder at any age, at least in comparison to the vast number of homicides committed by men. Historically, murderers of either sex have generally not been teenagers but adults over the age of eighteen (see Figure 1.1). However, in recent years, this traditional profile of the American murderer has been undergoing a relentless and troublesome change.

Before 1990, well over 80 percent of all murders were committed by adults—individuals over the age of eighteen. However, beginning in the mid-1980s, the number of teenagers who committed homicide began to rise, while the number of adults who murdered began to decline. Now, as we approach the new millennium, the number of murderers under the age of eighteen represents approximately one-fifth of the total number of known killers in America. Given the large number of children who will reach their teenage years in the

Figure 1.2
Sex of Known Murder Offenders in the U.S.

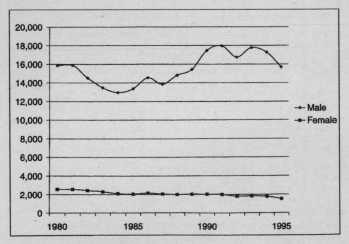

Source: Snyder and Finnegan.

next decade, it seems that our country will continue to experience a steady increase in the number of murders committed by adolescents, well into the next century. The implications of this changing profile of the American murderer are frightening and profound, especially given the changing demographics of our nation as a whole.

As in the past, most future murders will probably be committed by men (see Figure 1.2). However, the average age of the killers is declining, and today the perpetrator of this crime is more likely to be a teenager than ever before in our history. Also, unlike the experience of the past few decades, the victims of these killers have taken on a new and alarming profile; in recent years, the number of victims who were completely unknown to their murderer has been rising steadily. Now, at the end of the twentieth century, it is not uncommon for an individual to be slain by a youthful offender who had no personal relationship with his victim (see Figure 1.3). This new

Figure 1.3
Relationship of Known Murder Offenders to Victims in the U.S.

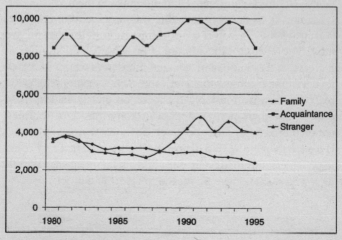

Source: Snyder and Finnegan.

trend of impersonal homicide does not bode well for the future of our nation.

In 1995, at least 3,800 teenagers between the age of thirteen and eighteen were formally arrested for murder in the United States. That number represented approximately 20 percent of all murder arrests in our nation, while the number of teenagers in that same age group represented only approximately 10 percent of our population. As disturbing as these statistics are, the Federal Bureau of Investigation (FBI), which published this information, believes that they are conservative. Since this data is collected solely from voluntary reports from law enforcement agencies across the United States, it is very likely that the number of teenagers arrested for murder each year is persistently understated.

These statistics may be an ominous vision of the new millennium, if we do not take hold of this problem with both a massive national effort and many deeply personal changes at the family level. It is possible that the decades ahead will be darkened by an increasing number of murders committed by a burgeoning youthful population, an ever-growing number of whose victims are unrelated and unknown to them.

However, as horrifying as this vision of the future may be, it is avoidable. To begin to set things right in this nation, we must first *recognize* the imminent possibility of a significant increase in the number of teenage murderers who will attack their victims for impersonal and sometimes incomprehensible reasons. Then we must clearly focus on understanding these crimes and their perpetrators. Certainly, this is a looming national crisis that must be given our most serious attention. If we are to avoid such a disturbing future, we must first come to an understanding of why our children kill—especially children who seem to have no reason to resort to murder.

THE UNCERTAINTY ABOUT ADOLESCENTS WHO KILL

In 1995 the Federal Bureau of Investigation estimated that well over two million juveniles under the age of eighteen were arrested, on a variety of charges that ranged in seriousness from curfew violations to murder. This represented an increase of more than 30 percent over the total number of teenagers arrested a decade previous to the FBI report (see Table 1.1). While the total number of adult arrests increased over the ten-year period (from 1986 to 1995) by some 14 percent, the rate at which juveniles were arrested saw more than double that increase.

Even more alarming than the increasing number of our children who are arrested each year is the number of those juveniles who are subsequently charged with extremely violent crimes, such as murder or non-negligent manslaughter. Since 1986 the number of juveniles arrested for violent crimes has increased by nearly a third, while the number arrested for murder has escalated by over two-thirds. This stunning increase in arrests occurred during a period in which the overall number of arrests for violent crimes committed by adults slowed, and the number of arrests for murder by adults actually dropped slightly (see Table 1.1). To compound this bleak scenario, it is known that these statistics are conservative. Unfortunately, however, the extent to which the number of adolescent arrests over the past decade is understated cannot be accurately determined.

Table 1.1
Ten-Year Trend in Arrests (1986–1995)

Arrests	Under 18	18 and Over
Percentage increase in total arrests	30.1	14.2
Percentage increase in arrests for violent crimes	67.3	31.4
Percentage increase in arrests for murder	89.9	−0.3

Source: U.S. Federal Bureau of Investigation, *Uniform Crime Report: 1995* (Washington, DC: 1996).

When we examine the FBI statistics for the number of children arrested for violent crimes more closely, we can begin to develop a clearer profile of the contemporary juvenile offender. These statistics indicate that relatively few children under the age of fourteen commit a violent crime. However, beginning at age fourteen, and continuing through age eighteen, the number of violent crimes committed by juveniles becomes significant. This data indicates that a child of fourteen is nearly as likely to commit a violent crime as an individual of eighteen (see Figure 1.4). The troubling conclusion is that once a child has reached the age of fourteen, he or she is as likely to commit a violent crime as an individual who would be considered an adult in every state in this nation. From a statistical point of view, there is little variation with age in the probability of the commission of a violent crime once a child has reached his or her teenage years. In essence, younger

Figure 1.4
Age Distribution of Children Arrested for Violent Crimes in 1995 (FBI estimates)

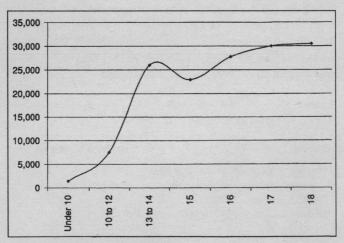

Source: Federal Bureau of Investigation.

adolescents can be, and often are, as violent as older teenagers or young adults.

However, recent arrest statistics for the ultimate form of violent crime—murder—indicate a somewhat different profile for the juvenile offender. Children under the age of fourteen rarely commit murder, although this does occasionally occur. Once a child reaches his or her fourteenth birthday, there is a steadily increasing possibility that his or her arrest for a violent crime will be for murder or non-negligent homicide. Once a juvenile embarks on a path of violence and runs afoul of the law, he becomes more likely to murder as he gets older (see Figure 1.5). By the time he reaches his eighteenth birthday, he or she is approximately three times more likely to commit murder than a youngster of fourteen or fifteen. In this sense, older teenagers and young adults more often turn to the ultimate form of violence than do younger adolescents.

Figure 1.5
Age Distribution of Children Arrested for Murder in 1995 (FBI estimates)

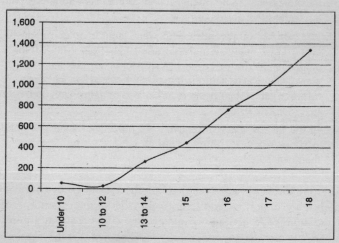

Source: Federal Bureau of Investigation.

In 1996, the Department of Justice issued a report on juvenile offenders in the United States that added troubling but more complete elements to the profile of young perpetrators of extremely violent crimes:[1]

- The number of juvenile murderers tripled in the ten years between 1984 and 1994. This is a trend that is expected to continue until at least the year 2010, based primarily on the large number of children who will be entering their teenage years over the next decade or so.

- By 1994, 80 percent of juvenile murderers used a firearm, whereas only 50 percent had done so a decade earlier, clearly indicating a more ready access to lethal weapons and a greater willingness to use them in the commission of violent crimes. The availability and use of these weapons directly contributes to the number of homicides in America.

- Thirty percent of all juvenile murderers had an adult accomplice to their crime.

- The proportion of juveniles who killed in groups rose to 55 percent in 1994 from 43 percent in 1980. This escalation reflects the increased activity of gangs, now found in communities both large and small across our nation.

- The number of juveniles who were *victims* of homicide increased by 82 percent in the decade 1984–1994. Many of these victims were murdered by individuals under the age of eighteen. This clearly demonstrates that more of our children are turning against their peers in lethal acts of aggression then ever before in our history.

- In the fifteen years since 1980, 93 percent of Caucasian and African-American murder victims were slain by a person of their own race.

Although statistics surrounding the violent crimes of juveniles are important and help to provide an understanding of the aggressive actions of our children, they pale in significance to the fundamental issue of *why* so many of these young people resort to violence and murder. Sadly, despite decades of effort on a broad front in this country, we still cannot answer this question with certainty. In many instances, we simply do not know why our children kill.

However, our knowledge of this issue is slowly improving, and there is reason for optimism. Behaviorists can now point with some assurance to a variety of factors that are shared by many extremely violent children, including those who kill:[2]

- A history of abuse in childhood
- Father figures may be absent, non-nurturing, or passive
- Mothers may be dominant, overprotective, or seductive
- Violence is expressed in the home and throughout childhood
- Children experience a deep sense of abandonment and distrust
- Family environment is unstable and often in turmoil
- Mothers may experience fear of their children

A large percentage of these violent juveniles have experienced a horrendous childhood and have been subjected to identifiable adverse factors, such as debilitating poverty, physical and sexual abuse, a violent family environment, or abandonment or rejection. Background influences and experiences such as these are generally considered to be precursors to juvenile violence and are often discovered in the history of children who eventually go on to commit murder.

From time to time, additional studies have been undertaken in an effort to understand why children commit specific types of violent crime, such as the murder of one or both of their parents. As in the case of juveniles who commit other extremely violent crimes, there appear to be indicators, or precursors, to violence that a significant percentage of these youth share in their backgrounds:[3]

- Indications of physical abuse by one or both parents
- Evidence of parental sexual stimulation of the child

- Evidence of overattachment to the mother
- Absent father figure

However, despite the tantalizing nature of much of this research, none of it has proven definitive.

Over time, we have developed a general familiarity with some of the key elements often found in the profile of a juvenile murderer. When a child is deprived of a stable home life, proper nurturing, a safe family environment, and freedom from violence at home and on the street, he or she may be more prone to acting out in a violent way than his more fortunate, economically advantaged counterparts. We have also learned that the factors outlined above often play a significant role in the histories of violent juveniles. However, as Tony Crespi and Sandra Rigazio-DiGillo point out in their assessment of recent studies of juvenile violence, researchers have yet to come to a consensus about the fundamental family dynamics and experiences in childhood that so often seem to play a major role in the later crimes of these children:

Overall, the literature on adolescent murderers is disappointingly meager in light of the increasing violence attributed to juveniles. Of [the] approximately 50 studies, which have been published involving adolescent homicide, none have focused specifically on family dynamics.[4]

It is important to realize that none of these predisposing factors, whether general or specific, guarantee that a child will grow up to be violent. In fact, there are literally tens of millions of children in America who experience these same horrors in childhood and never act out violently. Also, there are a growing number of juveniles who have apparently never experienced any of these negative factors in their childhood but have committed the most gruesome and violent crimes.

Certainly, many of us are now at least somewhat familiar with those elements thought to be common to so many violent youth. Reports of gang-related violence in America's largest cities are pervasive, disturbing, and frightening. Media accounts of rape, robbery, and murder committed by teenagers are daily fare in most of the densely populated areas of our nation, and even in the presumed safety of our most prestigious and affluent suburbs. Violent crime associated with drug-related activities is pervasive, and it leaves few American communities untouched. However, there are other violent crimes committed by our children that seem enigmatic and inexplicable, at least in terms of the motivation of the perpetrator.

From time to time, we learn of a murder committed by a juvenile that does not fit with what we have come to expect of violent crimes in general. We may read of a child who has murdered a stranger, simply to experience the thrill of the crime; or we may watch a television report about a teenager who has slain a lifelong friend for reasons that even he cannot fully understand or explain. When we learn of these crimes we are shocked and afraid, because this violence seems to have no basis in our experience. These seem to be acts without any comprehensible motivation. For these crimes, we can find no predisposing factors to violence, and we are unable to come to a satisfactory, understandable conclusion. Still, we each recognize that these seemingly motiveless murders have become more common in recent years, just as our growing population of adolescent citizens has become more violent in general.

When we read reports of children who murder without reason, the information we receive about their crimes rarely deals with the motivations and background of the perpetrators. Sadly, these reports often tell us only what we already know— that our children are becoming more violent and that they are apparently doing so for reasons that seem less and less comprehensible. We are persistently left with the same, unanswered question: *why do these children kill?* Why do these unlikely perpetrators, these children who clearly meet our definition of "good kids," commit such inconceivable crimes?

NOTES

1. U.S. Department of Justice, "Juvenile Offenders and Victims: 1996 Update on Violence," U.S. Department of Justice (Internet Edition), 1 June 1996.

2. Tony D. Crespi and Sandra A. Rigazio-DiGillo, "Adolescent Homicide and Family Pathology: Implications for Research and Treatment With Adolescents," *Adolescence* (Internet Edition), 1 June 1996.

3. Ibid.

4. Ibid.

2

FEAR, DENIAL, AND MURDER

> No passion so effectively robs the mind of all its powers of
> acting and reasoning as fear.
>
> Edmund Burke
> *The Origin of Our Ideas of the Sublime and Beautiful*

The United States Justice Department estimates that at least
three to four hundred infants die each year because they are
discarded or slain by their mothers immediately after birth.[1] In
truth, the number of infants who die in this way is probably
much greater. As in the case of the actual number of adolescent and adult homicides in America, we simply do not know
the number of murder victims who are infants. To date no
agency or organization has been able to gather reliable and
meaningful statistics about this troubling issue. Often these
deaths are brought to light only with the discovery of the remains of the tiny, unfortunate victims, who frequently remain
unclaimed and unidentified.

Many of these infants were stillborn at birth and were discarded in a moment of panic or indifference by their mothers.
However, many others died from exposure after having been
abandoned while still alive and viable. Sadly, a significant and
growing number of newborns are willfully and brutally murdered each year, frequently at the hands of a young mother.

Of those infants who are deliberately slain by their mothers, many were born to unwed teenagers, who killed them
immediately after delivery. Although not a common form of
violence in America, this crime has occurred with sufficient

regularity to be formally recognized as a unique category of murder. In 1970 Dr. Phillip J. Resnick, a forensic psychologist at University Hospital of Cleveland and a nationally recognized expert on the murder of newborns, coined a new word for this kind of unthinkable violence: *neonaticide*. By definition, neonaticide means the killing of an infant within twenty-four hours of his or her birth.

Although not unique to unwed teenage mothers, neonaticide is often associated in the press and in the mind of the public with these juveniles. When such a crime comes to light it sometimes garners sensational media coverage, leaving the reader with a profound sense of astonishment and disbelief at the apparent callous disregard for life exhibited by the murderer. Compounding the shock of this crime is the growing realization that neonaticide is a crime that regularly cuts across all segments of our society, often occurring without any correlation to the social or economic conditions of the young perpetrator.

Even though this type of murder has been traditionally associated with adolescents whose childhood was marred by poverty, violence, abuse, and the lack of an adequate education, neonaticide also occurs among teenagers reared in prosperous, well-educated, and stable family environments. However, regardless of the social or economic differences in the backgrounds of the teenagers who murder their newborns, these juveniles often share identifiable patterns of behavior. For instance, the teenage mother who murders her infant probably has no history of violence or criminal violations of the law before she commits her crime. She generally makes no significant attempt to arrange for the abortion of her pregnancy, and she typically works with diligence (and success) to hide her pregnancy from her parents and other adults. These teenagers typically struggle with a sense of loneliness, guilt, and isolation that is profound, overwhelming, and usually unmanageable, yet they are unwilling or unable to seek out support from those closest to them.

In the majority of cases in which a mother kills her newborn, two recognizable and apparently contradictory elements are at the forefront of her violent behavior. Together, these elements can combine with sufficient volatility to impel her toward murder:

- Fear of the birth of her child and the impending, seemingly overwhelming, responsibilities of motherhood, which signal the collapse of her adolescent life as she knows it
- Strong, often insurmountable, denial of her own pregnancy.

In this confluence of overwhelming emotional forces, fear directly contributes to the adolescent's eventual ability to commit the brutal crime, while denial disassociates her from a heinous act that she would otherwise be unwilling even to consider (see Table 2.1).

When the day of her baby's birth finally arrives, it may seem that the young mother has already made a conscious decision to murder her newborn, since she has failed to accept any of the other options that, to us, seem so obvious and reasonable. In truth, the perpetrator's incredible act of violence is not so simple or well planned. When she does lash out in this final moment of horror, it is almost always her first significant act of violence against another human being. In this sense, it is an unexpected, terrifying moment of fatal aggression that is sometimes as incomprehensible to the juvenile murderer as it is to those who later learn of the deed. When the teenage mother murders her infant, it is rarely, if ever, anything but a desperate act that horrifyingly demonstrates her unshakable conviction that, to her, there *were* no other options. If it is not such an obvious act of desperation, then it can only be one of insanity.

The murder of a newborn by his or her mother is considered by behaviorists, law enforcement personnel, psychologists, researchers, and child-welfare advocates to be one of the most complex and frustrating categories of crime in our society,

Table 2.1
Some Signs and Symptoms of Denial

Areas Affected	Symptoms
Perception and Attention	The individual appears dazed and confused, demonstrates selective inattention, and exhibits the inability to appreciate the significance of obvious stimuli.
Consciousness	There is evidence of amnesia (partial or total), and the individual exhibits a failure to experience obvious events.
Processing of Ideas	The individual disavows the meaning of stimuli and there is a loss of reality and appropriateness of thought (by disavowal). The individual appears incapable of organizing his or her thoughts.
Emotions	There is evidence of numbness and a lack of appropriate emotional response to most or all stimuli. In some instances, there is a complete absence of emotional response.
Somatic Manifestations	The individual exhibits clear symptoms of tension-related inhibition.
Actions and Activities	Behavior can vary radically and can range from frantic overactivity to complete isolation and withdrawal.

Source: H. H. Goldman, ed., *Review of General Psychiatry* (Norwalk, CT: Appleton and Lange, 1988), 41.

in terms both of understanding and prevention. It is arguably one of the most troubling and least comprehensible forms of violence, because it throws into question our essential understanding of such vital and profoundly personal issues as parenting, love, and responsibility to those who are completely dependent on us for their lives. The impact of this crime is pervasive, and it is especially meaningful to those of us who are parents. We are compelled to try to understand how an adolescent can arrive at such a pitch of fear and dissociation with the life within her body that she is capable of committing an act of such unsurpassed brutality and callousness.

A SOLITARY, INTIMATE CRIME

In the majority of cases of neonaticide, the murderer slays her child in secret and in an intensely personal but extremely brutal manner. It is this common scenario of solitary, intimate, and extreme violence that, in part, lends such a sense of horror to these acts of murder. However, these patterns also help us to somewhat understand the complex motivations of the murderer and recognize the overwhelming crisis that must be confronted by a pregnant adolescent who cannot successfully assume the awesome responsibilities of her situation.

In January 1986, a sixteen-year-old Wisconsin teenager gave birth after an eight-month pregnancy, which she was able to conceal from her parents and other adults. The adolescent gave birth alone, in her parents' home, and immediately killed her newborn by multiple stab wounds. She then wrapped her baby's body in a plastic bag and hid it in the garage of the family home. When the body was finally discovered, police were summoned. They searched the rest of the home, located the knife used by the young murderer, took her into custody, and charged her with first-degree murder. She was subsequently ordered to stand trial as a juvenile and pleaded guilty to one count of second-degree murder. The teenager was eventually sentenced to one-year imprisonment in a state detention facility. When questioned as to her motive for murdering her newborn, the adolescent said that she was desperately afraid of what those around her, especially her parents, would think of her if they discovered that she was pregnant.[2]

A similar case took place in New York, on July 10, 1988, in

an affluent upstate family home. A fifteen-year-old girl in her second year of high school gave birth alone to a full-term baby boy. After giving birth she carefully cleaned the infant, wrapped him in a towel, and placed him in a plastic garbage bag. Incredibly, the teenager then took the bundle and threw it down a steep embankment outside the family home. The infant suffered massive head injuries from the fall and was found several hours later by a neighbor. The baby died before he was able to receive medical treatment.

Once again, as in the Wisconsin case, none of the family members were aware of the teenager's pregnancy. The girl was arrested, charged with second-degree murder, and sent to trial as a juvenile. Her only explanation for the murder was that she was terrified of what she believed her mother's reaction would be to her pregnancy.[3]

In both the Wisconsin and New York homicides the teenage perpetrator was able to hide her pregnancy from those around her, give birth to her baby alone and unaided, and murder the newborn in an especially brutal, gruesome manner. In both cases the murderers claimed a paralyzing fear of what their parents (or other adults) would think of their pregnancy. Both teenagers faced the awesome responsibility of parenthood alone, and neither was able to resolve the situation before she gave birth.

It goes without saying that both mothers denied the reality and true meaning of their pregnancies and that both avoided confronting the issue with the aid of those who could have provided support or assistance. Neither of these teenagers had a violent or criminal history, and both were consumed with the disappointment they believed they had wrought upon their families. These strong beliefs are overwhelmingly common to pregnant teenage girls who later go on to murder their newborns. They are the essential ingredients in a lethal cocktail of fear and denial, which so often forms the basis for neonaticide.

However, there are certainly other motivations for neonaticide committed by teenagers. Poverty and ignorance are sometimes the insurmountable issues that result in murder. In 1987, in California, a fifteen-year-old girl secretly gave birth in her parents' home after hiding her pregnancy for nine months. When she was fourteen, this same teenager had given birth to her first baby and had been told by her parents that if she ever became pregnant again she would have to leave the family home. There simply was not enough income for her parents to support any more children. However, the young girl *did* become pregnant again and was in constant fear of losing her only support if her parents discovered her condition.

On October 9, 1987, immediately after giving birth to a full-term infant, the young mother placed her newborn in a plastic bag and threw the bag into a nearby Dumpster. The baby subsequently died from suffocation. The young mother was arrested and charged with murder; she quickly pleaded guilty. She was later sentenced to one year's imprisonment in the Los Angeles County Juvenile Center.[4]

Even in this case, where the harsh realities of poverty played a dominant role in the young mother's decision to commit murder, it is obvious that elements of shame, fear, and denial were pervasive and fundamental. This confluence of emotional forces is predominant in cases of neonaticide committed by adolescent mothers, regardless of the differences in their economic backgrounds.

On July 7, 1997, Elizabeth Vargas, host of the American Broadcasting Company's program *Good Morning America*, interviewed a young woman who had been forced to face the same crisis as the three teenage mothers just profiled. Four years before the telecast Katherine Destefano had become pregnant, at the age of eighteen. Destefano had been able to conceal the pregnancy from her parents until nearly the date of her baby's birth. However, unlike many teenagers who commit neonaticide, Destefano had decided to keep her baby. When interviewed by Vargas she provided a profound insight into the feelings she had about her pregnancy—feelings that are over-whelmingly common among pregnant teenagers:

Vargas: Why did you keep your pregnancy a secret?

Destefano: When I found out I was pregnant, I was very, very scared. I was eighteen [and] I was just out of high school. I had my world ahead of me. I was going to go to college. To become pregnant at such a young age, and being unprepared, you know, I was just a kid myself.

Vargas: Do you think you were in denial about it?

Destefano: I was.

Vargas: Were you hoping this really wasn't true?

Destefano: I was. Yes, I took two or three pregnancy tests before I actually believed I was pregnant. I was in denial. I realized I was pregnant. It was the type of thing, though, you put it in the back of your mind, you don't think about it and it'll go away.

Vargas: Why didn't you tell anybody, any of your family members, any of your friends?

Destefano: I was just scared. I was ashamed. Everyone stresses so much that a young woman is not supposed to get pregnant, a young single woman, that it should not happen and it's bad. And I felt ashamed. I felt like I'd be made fun of, you know.[5]

The fears expressed by this teenage mother are typical, yet these overpowering emotional forces rarely lead to neonaticide. However, when fear, shame, and denial of their pregnancy become overwhelming and unanswerable factors in the lives of these adolescents, the scene can be set for unthinkable and unplanned violence. Phillip Resnick describes the confused and fearful state of mind of these pregnant teenagers in this way:

Sexually naïve from the start, they refuse to admit that they are pregnant. They've made no plans for the birth of their infant, either to keep it or to kill it. They fear discovery. They feel shame. And when their baby's first cry finally intrudes upon their denial, they want to silence it.[6]

The important, sometimes overpowering, role of fear, shame, and denial in the violent crimes of a pregnant adolescent has been acknowledged by many psychologists, psychiatrists, and behaviorists in recent years. One psychiatrist who has studied numerous cases of neonaticide is Morris Brozovsky, an assistant professor of psychiatry at State University's Downtown Medical Center in Brooklyn, New York. According to Brozovsky, young mothers who murder their newborns often act without a complete awareness of the impact of their violence: "And then there is a group [of adolescents] that will deny that they are pregnant until the delivery, and the stress of the delivery will put them into a brief psychotic state."[7]

In many cases of neonaticide defense attorneys point out the possibility that their clients were incapable of understanding the nature and impact of their acts when they murdered their newborns. They point out that this aberrant mental condition was due in large part to the overwhelming emotional forces inherent in their pregnant condition. In such cases the argument is made that the uncontrollable, fearful emotional state of the adolescent, combined with an unshakable denial of their pregnancy, represents significant mitigating circumstances in considering the legal culpability of their clients. Over the past decade this line of defense has been used with varying degrees of success, depending on the nature of the criminal circumstances, the background of the accused, the degree to which a deficient psychological state could be proven, and the jurisdiction in which the case was tried.

Over seven years ago, this line of defense was used in the case of Amy Ellwood. At the age of seventeen Ellwood thought she had been able to hide her pregnancy from most of those around her. Eventually she gave birth to a viable baby boy, alone and unaided, in the family home. She then wrapped her newborn in towels and plastic bags, placed him in a plastic cooler, and threw the cooler into a nearby lake.

Despite the efforts of her attorney, when Ellwood was

finally brought to trial for her crime her line of defense proved unacceptable to the jury. In 1991, she was convicted of second-degree murder and sentenced to serve two to seven years in prison. However, during the course of the trial an extremely unusual circumstance was brought to light in Ellwood's case—a situation that was almost certainly a contributing factor in the murder of her newborn, although it played no role in her defense. It was disclosed that the teenager's parents, a high school principal (father) and a teacher (mother), had actually been aware of their daughter's pregnancy but refused to confront Amy with the issue, because they feared losing her.[8]

A year after Amy Ellwood committed her crime, Stephanie Wernick gave birth to a baby, also alone and unaided, in a dormitory bathroom on the campus of Long Island University, New York. After the birth she stuffed several wads of toilet paper down the newborn's throat, wrapped the infant in a plastic bag, and disposed of the body in a garbage container. In 1993 Wernick went to trial, charged with the crime of manslaughter.

As in the Ellwood case, Wernick's attorney used a defense argument based on fear, shame, and denial. In addition, her attorney portrayed Wernick as a person of low I.Q. who had

---

Snapshot Profile of Amy Ellwood

A seventeen-year-old, who had no history of violence or criminal activities. After believing that she had hidden her pregnancy from her parents and other adults, Ellwood gave birth to a baby boy in her family home. Immediately after his delivery, the teenager placed the infant in a cooler and threw it into a nearby lake. Her defense at trial was based on a diminished state of mind due to her pregnancy. However, the jury found her guilty of second-degree murder, and she was eventually sentenced to serve two to seven years in prison.

been forced to compete (unsuccessfully) in a family that was extremely achievement oriented. Wernick's defense tactic came to be known as the "neonaticide syndrome" in the press, but it was only allowed to be partially presented to the jury during her trial.[9] However, the jury that heard her case apparently believed at least the portion of the defense argument it was allowed to consider and threw out the original charge of manslaughter, finding Wernick guilty of the lesser charge of criminally negligent homicide. Nearly six years after Wernick committed her crime, she had exhausted her appeals and began serving a sentence of one to four years in prison.

In both the Ellwood and Wernick cases defense attorneys claimed that their clients had completely denied their pregnancy and were so fearful and distraught after giving birth that they were incapable of fully understanding the nature of their criminal acts. However, despite this increasingly popular defense tactic, the vast majority of teenagers who commit neonaticide are eventually found to be legally aware of their actions and thus guilty, although sometimes with mitigating circumstances that are reflected in lesser charges or reduced prison sentences.

Snapshot Profile of Stephanie Wernick

A college teenager, who had no history of violence or criminal activities. She gave birth to her baby, alone and unaided, in a college dormitory room. After the delivery Wernick stuffed wads of toilet paper down the infant's throat, bound him in a plastic bag, and discarded the body in a garbage container. When she was tried for her crime, Wernick's defense team used an argument of "neonaticide syndrome" to explain her actions. The jury that heard Wernick's case threw out the original charge of manslaughter and found her guilty of the lesser crime of negligent homicide. She was sentenced to serve a term of one to four years in prison.

FRIGHTENED TEENAGERS OR
MURDERERS WITHOUT CONSCIENCES?

At the end of 1996 and again in the summer of 1997 two cases of neonaticide claimed massive and compelling headlines in the press and on television. Although in many ways these crimes were similar to those committed by numerous other adolescents each year, their details sent a profound wave of horror and disbelief across our nation. This stunned public reaction was due in part to the relentless and often extravagant press coverage of the murders. However, there was another aspect to these homicides that could not help but draw our national attention: in both cases, the adolescents who allegedly murdered their newborns seemed to be universally recognized as "good kids"—teenagers whose moments of unparalleled viciousness seemed well beyond comprehension and wholly inexplicable, particularly in light of what came to be known of their backgrounds.

Also capturing our national conscience, in the case of Amy Grossberg and Brian Peterson, Jr., was the fact that the newborn was allegedly murdered in the presence of both the adolescent mother and father, leaving us uncertain about the roles each of these individuals may have played in the infant's death. The participation of both the mother and father in the murder of a newborn is in itself extremely rare and inherently disturbing. On March 9, 1998, Peterson pleaded guilty to manslaughter in the case. Less than a month later, Grossberg entered the same plea in a separate proceeding. Both teenagers have now been sentenced to prison.

The case of Melissa Drexler has not been settled; therefore, it is vital that no assumptions be made about her guilt or innocence at this point. However, the horror and sadness of these cases and the impact of the crimes on the accused adolescents and their families represent two stories that cannot be ignored, because they are so deeply personal and important to an understanding of our children. Perhaps in some way the unfortunate sagas of these teenagers can lead us to a better understanding of this kind of senseless violence.

"An Ideal Young Couple"

Amy Grossberg was once described by her attorney as a "dream daughter."[10] Few, if any, who knew this pleasant teenager would have disagreed with that assessment. Amy was raised in a loving, well-respected family and had been known throughout her life by friends and neighbors as a youngster who was intelligent, polite, naturally artistic, outgoing, and happy. She lived in a family home that was valued at nearly a million dollars, situated on two sprawling acres in an up-scale, prestigious community in New Jersey. Grossberg's father, Alan, owned his own business (a furniture store), and her mother, Sonye, was a successful interior designer and devoted mother. According to all accounts, the Grossberg family was caring and close knit, the parents providing abundant love and support to each other and their daughter, Amy.

By the time she was a junior in high school, Amy had blossomed into a pretty, delicate teenager and had fallen in love with Brian Peterson, Jr., a handsome, athletic, and likeable adolescent whose background was also prosperous and seemingly flawless. Neither Amy Grossberg nor Brian Peterson, Jr., had any history of violence or problems with the law. They were

Snapshot Profile of Amy Grossberg

A stable, artistic, and happy eighteen-year-old freshman in college who came from an affluent background and a close family environment. She had no criminal record and no history of violence. Amy was able to hide her pregnancy from her parents until she gave birth to a baby boy. On April 22, 1998, Grossberg pleaded guilty to a charge of manslaughter in the death of her baby.

in every sense ideal teenagers who had each been reared in stable, comfortable family environments.

As a boy, Brian Peterson, Jr., attended Otsego Elementary School and Candlewood Middle School in the comfortable community of Dix Hills, New Jersey. While at middle school Peterson demonstrated good promise as an athlete and was on both the soccer and wrestling teams. In 1992 the youngster moved to his mother's affluent, two-story home and enrolled at Ramapo High School in Wyckoff, New Jersey. It was there that he met Amy Grossberg.

Both Peterson and Grossberg enjoyed stable, close, and affluent home lives throughout their high school years. Both were intelligent and successful in school, and they each developed and followed their unique, individual interests. Amy pursued her love of art with a passion, and Brian dedicated himself to athletic competition. It was obvious to all who knew the couple that Amy and Brian were very devoted to each other and seemingly destined to experience a long, happy future together.

In their junior year, the couple began dating regularly and spending significant amounts of time together. They attended the Ramapo High School junior and senior proms together, while independently they continued to develop their special talents. By his junior year Peterson had become a recognized and successful high school athlete, while Grossberg demonstrated a promising and obvious artistic talent that she hoped would continue to develop through pursuit of an art major in college. However, by the time of her senior prom Amy Grossberg was several weeks pregnant, and the couple was faced with the first serious crisis of their young lives, although they were careful to not let anyone else know about Amy's condition.

After his graduation from high school Peterson enrolled as a freshman at Gettysburg College in Pennsylvania, a three-hour drive from the University of Delaware, where Grossberg was also enrolled as a freshman. During the summer before her first year of college, when she was surely aware of her pregnancy, Grossberg worked with five-year-olds at the Wyckoff YMCA. Throughout that summer, as had been her lifelong pattern, Amy showed a significant talent for art and a cheerful willingness to work with her young charges. While Amy worked with the YMCA, Brian Peterson spent the summer playing golf and involving himself in other athletic activities. Most summer evenings the couple was together, often spending time at the Grossbergs' private country club. Even by the end of summer, when it was time for the couple to go off to their respective campuses, no one else was apparently aware of Amy's condition. To all who knew the young couple, everything in their relationship seemed normal and upbeat. Their lives were just beginning to blossom—or so it seemed.

After Grossberg and Peterson arrived at their respective college campuses, they continued to see each other regularly, despite the three-hour drive that separated them. According to Grossberg's college acquaintances, Peterson was a frequent weekend visitor at the University of Delaware's Thompson Hall, where Amy had taken up residence. The couple also spoke to each other every night on the telephone. Throughout the first few months of the new school year, there was nothing to indicate that distance had affected Amy and Brian's obvious love for each other.

However, Amy's pregnant condition was becoming harder

Snapshot Profile of Brian Peterson, Jr.

A handsome, athletic eighteen-year-old and freshman in college who came from an affluent and close family. He had no criminal record and no history of violence. Together with Amy Grossberg, the pair hid her pregnancy from their parents and other adults. On March 9, 1998, Peterson pleaded guilty to a charge of manslaughter in the case.

and harder to conceal, especially with her small, one-hundred-pound frame. She changed her wardrobe to conceal her obvious physical condition and began to avoid the increasing questions and suggestions from her college acquaintances. To some, the usually happy, smiling teenager now seemed a bit preoccupied.

An acquaintance of Grossberg's who lived at Thompson Hall claims to have suspected Amy's pregnancy shortly after the school year began: "She never told anyone, but it was obvious. She wore baggy clothes to hide it."[11] Amy's friend also noticed that whenever fellow students asked Grossberg if she was pregnant, the freshman would strongly deny it—perhaps a bit too strongly. To a few of her new college friends, it seemed that Amy was becoming more withdrawn and troubled; however, her schoolmates were apparently reluctant to press the issue.

Regardless of the fear that may have secretly assailed her in those final months of her pregnancy, Amy Grossberg remained as popular on the university campus as she had been in high school. Those who knew her at the University of Delaware were shocked when they eventually learned of the crime for which she was arrested. Another freshman and acquaintance of Amy's who lived at Thompson Hall said this about Grossberg and the charges against her: "We are confused. She is just a great person. She was always smiling. You couldn't have made up a story like this because no one would have believed you."[12]

Brian Peterson, Jr., was also highly regarded by all who knew him at Gettysburg College, as well as by his friends and neighbors back home. One of the Peterson family's neighbors expressed the near-universal feelings about Amy and Brian: "They are both great kids. You could call them an ideal young couple. Both were smart and friendly. And they seemed so happy."[13]

However, despite the outward appearances of normalcy, by November things were falling apart for Amy and Brian. She had reached the end of her pregnancy, and neither of the adolescents had made plans for the future; nor had they shared the news of Amy's pregnancy with any adult who could provide counseling or assistance. The young couple was now faced with a decision that would irrevocably change their lives and those of their respective families.

On the evening of Monday, November 11, 1996, Amy Grossberg placed an urgent call to Brian Peterson at his dormitory residence and told him that she was going into labor. Peterson drove the three hours from Gettysburg College to the University of Delaware, arriving at Thompson Hall shortly after midnight to meet Grossberg and take her to a motel near her campus. Whether or not the couple had discussed any plans for that night is unknown. However, Brian took Amy from her dormitory room in his Toyota and headed into the night. Neither Amy nor Brian told Amy's roommate of their plans or their destination.

According to investigating officers, Amy Grossberg delivered her baby early on the morning of November 12, 1996, at a Comfort Inn near the University of Delaware campus, with Peterson by her side. The newborn was a boy, twenty inches long and weighing six pounds, two ounces. The two adolescents delivered him at approximately 4:00 A.M. in room 220 of the roadside motel. According to prosecutors, after the birth the infant was beaten about the head, shaken, stuffed into a gray garbage bag with yellow drawstrings, and deposited in a Dumpster outside the motel room. Grossberg and Peterson then slept for a few hours, and shortly before noon took the car they were driving to a nearby car wash, allegedly to remove any incriminating evidence. The following day, when police officials searched the motel grounds, they discovered the body of the infant in the motel Dumpster, still wrapped in the plastic garbage bag.

Later on November 12 Brian delivered Amy back to Thompson Hall. However, she soon began to suffer significant physical discomfort and bleeding. At about 5:30 that afternoon

Grossberg collapsed and was taken by ambulance to Christiana Hospital in Newark. She was diagnosed as suffering from complications of the birth twelve hours earlier: her body had failed to expel the placenta. Attending physicians quickly realized that Grossberg had given birth to a baby within the previous day and began to question her. She readily admitted the delivery of a son and provided details that would quickly bring police into the case, lead to her own arrest and that of Brian Peterson on charges of murder, and forever destroy the lives of the young couple and their parents. During the course of her conversation with hospital officials Amy admitted that Brian Peterson, Jr., was the father of the infant and had been with her at the time of the boy's birth.

Checking on her statements, police soon located incriminating physical evidence that supported their worst fears. They discovered bloodied bed linens left behind in Amy's dormitory room that linked her to the recent birth of her baby. Investigating officers also interviewed Grossberg's roommate, who told them about Brian Peterson's late arrival at Thompson Hall the preceding evening and the couple's hasty and unexplained departure together. The gruesome picture of what had occurred in a nondescript Newark motel room earlier that morning was becoming clear. By this time, Brian Peterson, Jr., implicated by Grossberg's statements, had become the subject of intense interest by local authorities.

After leaving the Comfort Inn and delivering Amy back to Thompson Hall, Peterson had driven directly back to Gettysburg College. Once there, he was approached by a dormitory advisor and security officer, who had already been contacted by local police. Peterson too made several incriminating statements, including his role in disposing of the newborn earlier that day. The statements he made to university personnel led law enforcement officials to conclude that Peterson had helped Grossberg with the delivery of their son and then wrapped the infant in a plastic bag and personally deposited him in the motel Dumpster.[14] In fact, by this time police were convinced that the couple had willfully murdered the infant immediately after his birth. A search of Peterson's room disclosed more soiled bed linens that were linked to the crime scene, a map of the Newark area, and a receipt for the White Glove Car Wash near the Comfort Inn Motel.

The initial medical examiner's report on the death of Amy Grossberg's infant noted that the boy had been delivered full term and alive. After birth the infant had suffered "multiple skull fractures, with injury to the brain, blunt-force head trauma and shaking."[15] The obvious conclusion drawn by authorities from the medical examiner's report was that the newborn had been beaten to death immediately after delivery. However, the report was not conclusive about whether the infant had been alive at the time he was placed in the Dumpster. This raised an important legal issue as to whether or not the newborn had been alive when his parents abandoned him. However, for many who read the press accounts of the birth and death of the baby, the moral implications of what had occurred at the Comfort Inn that morning were already beyond question.

On November 18, 1996, Amy Grossberg was formally arrested on suspicion of first-degree murder in the death of her baby. Shortly after her arrest Grossberg's attorney stated that he was convinced his client had committed no crime, but he refused to say anything further, offering no explanation as to how he believed the infant had died. When asked about Grossberg's motives in hiding her pregnancy and delivering her baby in a motel with Peterson, her attorney also refused to provide any details. However, at least one major newspaper covering the story claimed that Amy Grossberg "was terrified [that] her mother would find out she was pregnant."[16] It seems likely, if not certain, that the teenager was fraught with guilt, fear, and denial of her pregnancy, as is so prevalent in cases of adolescent-committed neonaticide.

Three days later, on November 21, 1996, Brian Peterson, Jr., surrendered himself to law enforcement authorities on outstanding charges of first-degree murder. For several days after the warrant for his arrest was issued Peterson had spent time in seclusion with his family while his attorney quietly arranged for the adolescent to turn himself in. Peterson's parents and lawyer accompanied the obviously distraught and frightened teenager to face law enforcement officers. As the entourage pushed its way into the Federal Bureau of Investigation offices in Wilmington, Delaware, the teenager was subjected to the raging anger of a group of onlookers, who had gathered in front of the building, some of them screaming "baby killer!"[17]

Like Amy Grossberg's attorney, Peterson's lawyer denied that his client had committed murder. However, that opinion had no weight with the New Jersey judicial system. At an afternoon bail hearing the presiding judge ordered that Brian Peterson, Jr., be kept in the prison infirmary for at least seventy-two hours for standard medical and psychological evaluations and then be held without bail on charges of murder—similar to what had already happened with Amy. Late that afternoon Superior Court Judge Henry DuPont Ridgely imposed a gag order on all attorneys involved in the case.

On November 22 the medical examiner released additional details of the autopsy performed on the infant, who had come to be known as "Baby Grossberg" in the media. A spokeswoman for the Delaware Department of Health and Social Services noted that "the autopsy showed it [Baby Grossberg] was a full-term, healthy baby boy. That means it was born alive after a full term, nine-month pregnancy."[18] This report indicated clear support for the prosecutor's contention that Grossberg and Peterson had deliberately murdered their newborn on the morning of November 12.

The following week both adolescents were still in custody and being held without bail. On November 26 both waived their right to a preliminary hearing on charges of first-degree murder, under an agreement with prosecutors in the case. Earlier in the week the grand jury had met to hear the case against the teenagers but had failed to return an indictment. Given this turn of events, there was speculation in the media about why their attorneys had advised the adolescents to waive their right to a preliminary hearing. Much of the speculation centered around the question of whether prosecutors would, in return for the defendants' waiver of rights, drop their plans to seek the death penalty against the couple. However, no decision was immediately announced.

On December 9 the case against Amy Grossberg and Brian Peterson, Jr., was formally presented to the grand jury, which quickly returned indictments against the couple for first-degree murder. At the time of the grand jury decision Amy and Brian were still in prison, and prosecutors were reaffirming their position to seek the death penalty at trial. A week later, both Grossberg and Peterson formally entered pleas of innocent to the murder charges. At the preliminary hearing, defense requests for bail were denied; however, the presiding judge agreed to rehear the bail requests in a month's time.

During that initial hearing the couple's attorneys disclosed a possible line of defense, their contention that the infant had been brain damaged before birth. According to the defense argument, the adolescents were not only innocent of neonaticide but had not harmed their baby in any way. The defense claimed that Baby Grossberg had suffered from congenital brain damage before it was born, which had thrown the infant's viability into question. According to this theory, the baby had suffered from a birth defect that caused his brain to be split into two parts (schizencephaly).

Peterson's attorney, Jack Litman, declared, "Neither Amy nor Brian intended to cause nor in fact did cause any harm to the deceased."[19] However, defense attorneys would provide no further details about this position, which clearly contradicted the earlier information released by the medical examiner's office. Once again, press speculation was rampant, this time surrounding the question of legal maneuvering intended to induce prosecutors to consider a plea bargain for a lesser charge than first-degree murder.

One month later, on January 21, 1997, a second bail hearing was held in the case. This time the defense request was granted, and a bail of $300,000 for each defendant was imposed. In addition, the terms of bail required that Grossberg and Peterson relinquish their passports, live with their parents, wear electronic monitoring bracelets, and be subject to an early curfew each evening. However, the two defendants were not immediately released from prison. Rather, they were held for another week while arrangements were made for the out-of-state, electronic monitoring system that had been imposed by the judge.

By the end of the month both Amy Grossberg and Brian Peterson were back in New Jersey, in their parents' homes. Through their attorneys, both adolescents continued to deny that they had fractured their newborn's skull, while prosecutors remained adamant that they would seek the death penalty in a case they considered to be one of obvious and premeditated neonaticide.

In June 1997 the case against Amy Grossberg took a bizarre and unsettling twist: she unexpectedly agreed to an interview with television personality Barbara Walters on the ABC program *20/20*. This nationally aired television appearance was considered by some in the media as a clear ploy to present Grossberg in the best possible light and damage the prosecution's case against the couple. Others felt that Grossberg's interview with Walters was heart wrenching and sincere.

During the televised conversation Amy Grossberg made her legal position clear: "I would never hurt anything or anybody, especially something that would come from me."[20] When asked how she felt about facing the death penalty if convicted of the crime for which she had been earlier jailed, Grossberg answered: "Just hearing those words are terrifying."[21]

Also interviewed on *20/20* that evening was Sonye Grossberg, Amy's mother. Asked by Walters if she had known about her daughter's pregnancy, the elder Grossberg replied that she had seen Amy just two weeks before she gave birth but had no idea that she was pregnant. However, she went on to explain that she believed she knew *why* Amy had hidden her pregnancy but that she could not disclose it because of the gag order imposed in the case. This statement by Mrs. Grossberg initiated a legal controversy that directly impacted her daughter's defense and caused a furor among prosecutors.

Within three days of the telecast, prosecutors charged that the Walters/Grossberg interview had directly violated the gag order and had damaged the prosecution's strategy for trial. The New Jersey attorney general's office immediately filed a motion in Delaware Superior Court asking for sanctions against Amy Grossberg and her attorney, Robert Gottlieb. The motion charged that "certain factual matters were misrepresented by the participants during the course of the television broadcast" and that the program itself violated an earlier promise made by Grossberg's team of attorneys that their client would not undertake any television interviews.[22]

Because of the *20/20* interview and the strong objections raised by prosecutors, Amy Grossberg lost her attorney; Gottlieb was removed from the case by the presiding judge. Gottlieb tried to contest his dismissal, pointing out that in his opinion the original gag order did not apply to the defendants in the case, only the lawyers, and that therefore the sanctions against his participation as Grossberg's attorney should be lifted. Despite his arguments, the presiding judge denied all motions to reinstate the attorney.

The removal of Amy Grossberg's attorney was a blow to the young defendant and her family, who had come to value and trust Gottlieb's representation. Mr. and Mrs. Grossberg pleaded with the judge in writing to reinstate their daughter's attorney: "Not only has our daughter been hurt by this ruling [removing Gottlieb from the case], we are now faced with another dilemma. The only attorney who Amy trusted and felt secure with is no longer able to defend her in a court of law. We cannot understand why she can not have the attorney of her choice."[23] However, even the emotional appeal of Amy's distraught parents did nothing to change the judge's mind.

In early August 1997 matters became even more complicated for the Grossberg family when prosecutors subpoenaed Amy's parents to force them to disclose what they had known about their daughter's pregnancy. The source of information cited by the prosecutors in their motion was the infamous *20/20* television program that had aired in June. Sonye and Alan Grossberg were now to be dragged even deeper into the quagmire that seemed to surround every aspect of the morbid case.

Both Amy and Brian pleaded guilty to manslaughter the following spring, before their respective cases went to trial. In July 1998, Supreme Court Judge Henry DuPont Ridgely sentenced each to eight-year prison terms and a fine of $5,000. Ridgely subsequently suspended five and a half years of Grossberg's sentence and six years of Peterson's because he had cooperated with prosecutors in their case.

Regardless of the sentencing for Amy Grossberg and Brian Peterson, Jr., it is quite clear that this crime claimed far more than its original victim, Baby Grossberg. The lives of both adolescents and their families have been altered or destroyed forever, and in a way that can bring little possibility of eventual peace or happiness. Although the involvement of Brian Peterson, Jr., in the death of his son represents a rare and troubling exception to most cases of neonaticide, the overwhelming terror faced by Amy Grossberg in failing to deal with her pregnancy seems somehow understandable.

The fear, shame, and denial to which Amy succumbed may have directly led to her involvement in murder. If such was the case, we, as parents, are obligated to learn from this tragedy. We must work to recognize and understand the overwhelming emotional forces that can so suddenly and unexpectedly transform our nonviolent, caring children into potential murderers.

A Murderous Night at the Prom

Amy Grossberg and Brian Peterson, Jr., are not alone in being the most unlikely of murderers. In fact there are countless cases of adolescents with similarly stable, nonviolent backgrounds who have been accused of committing this most atrocious of crimes. One of them is another New Jersey teenager, by the name of Melissa Drexler.

Melissa was the only child of a close-knit, religious, middle-class family. Understandably, she quickly became the center of her parents' attention and love, and she remained so throughout her childhood and into her teenage years. Melissa was by any definition one of the "good kids," a child who apparently thrived in a positive and supportive home environment.

Around 1980, when Melissa was a toddler, the Drexlers moved from Bayonne to the Forked River section of Lacey Township, New Jersey. By 1996 the family was well established in this comfortable, quiet community. Melissa's childhood in Lacey Township was serene and uneventful, with her parents able and willing to provide all the love and physical comfort their daughter required. John Drexler, Melissa's father, worked in the computer industry, and her mother, Maria, worked at a local bank.

By all accounts, the Drexler family was close, well respected, and unremarkable. Like their daughter, Melissa's parents were quiet and unobtrusive, yet apparently happy and obviously devoted to their only child. One neighbor, who had known the Drexlers for a decade, described the family environment this way:

They really keep to themselves. They always have [kept to themselves], but they also made that little girl their whole lives. They worked around her schedule, took an active role in her education, and always went to school open houses. I do know that they are good parents. They're attentive and are always looking out for Melissa, who is a good kid and never got into trouble.[24]

At the age of eighteen, Melissa was a demure, delicate adolescent, weighing just over a hundred pounds. As a senior at the Lacey Township High School she was known to her classmates as a quiet, generous, and pleasant teenager who had enjoyed a close friendship with a handful of adolescents she had known since her early school years. By this time, Melissa was also deeply involved in a relationship with a boyfriend she had dated for over two years, John T. Lewis, Jr., of nearby Barnegat Township. Lewis, two years older than Drexler, was described by friends as quiet, serious, and obviously devoted to Melissa.

Neither Melissa nor John had any history of violence or conflict with the law, and both had made definite plans for their futures. After graduation from high school, Melissa was determined to attend Brookdale Community College, in Middletown Township, and eventually pursue a career in the fashion industry.

Like Amy Grossberg, Melissa Drexler had an impeccable reputation with neighbors and friends alike, although she was generally regarded as somewhat retiring and shy. A friend of Drexler's since the fourth grade described her as "a good person who would do anything for anyone."[25] That opinion seemed to be shared by all who knew her throughout her high school years. However, like Amy Grossberg, Melissa Drexler had a deep and abiding secret in her senior year—she was pregnant.

Despite her long-standing relationship, none of Melissa's friends suspected that she was carrying a child. In fact, according to several of Drexler's friends not even John, her boyfriend of over two years and the father of her unborn child, was aware of her pregnancy. Certainly her parents did not know. However, all of that would abruptly change in an evening of horrible tragedy at Melissa's high school prom. The adolescent mother and her family would be devastated by her actions that night, and an innocent life would be sacrificed.

The Lacey Township High School senior prom was a formal affair, scheduled to be held at the Garden Manor banquet hall in Aberdeen Township on Friday, June 6, 1997. It was also designed to be a festive and crowded event, with more than 350 people in attendance. The high school students were excited about the prom, which had become an honored tradition in the area. This year, prom-goers looked forward to the senior class theme for the evening, "I Will Remember You." As expected, Melissa Drexler and John Lewis had arranged to attend the dance together.

As soon as Drexler and Lewis arrived at the prom, at around 7:00 P.M., she left him and went directly to the women's restroom. During the drive to the banquet hall Melissa had complained of stomach cramps, so her date was not surprised when she immediately left him among their classmates, telling him that she would be back shortly. In a banquet hall restroom stall, after a secret, nine-month pregnancy, Melissa struggled alone to give birth to a baby boy. At birth the infant weighed six pounds, six ounces.

After delivering her baby, Melissa placed the infant into a plastic bag that she had retrieved from a sanitary-napkin receptacle, tightly knotted the top of the bag, and disposed of the bundle in a garbage container inside the restroom. She then returned to the prom to join her boyfriend and other classmates.

Snapshot Profile of Melissa Drexler

An eighteen-year-old high school senior who had a long-standing relationship with her boyfriend. Melissa came from a stable, loving family environment and was generally known as a quiet, happy adolescent. She had no criminal record and no history of violence. Melissa was able to hide her pregnancy from her parents, other adults, and the father of her baby. On the night of her senior prom, the teenager gave birth to her baby in a restroom, alone and unaided. After the delivery, she murdered the infant, discarded the body in a trash receptacle, and returned to the prom.

The total time that elapsed from when Melissa left her boy-friend and returned to the dance floor to rejoin him was not more than thirty minutes.

Reportedly, Melissa's behavior immediately after giving birth and rejoining her classmates was at best bizarre and certainly difficult to explain: "She asked the disk jockey [entertaining the prom attendees] to play her favorite Metallica song and danced with her boyfriend. A student told a reporter later, 'She seemed to be enjoying herself.' "[26] According to information later released by investigating authorities, Drexler also ate a salad and chatted in an animated way with several of her high school friends, acting in what appeared to be a completely normal fashion. However, some of Melissa's alleged activities after the birth of her son are in dispute. What is generally not contested is that the adolescent gave no indication of distress and in fact seemed to those who encountered her after she returned from the restroom to behave normally.

Had other students at the prom not noticed blood on the floor of the restroom and alerted a banquet hall maintenance man, no one would have guessed that this quiet teenager had just given birth to a baby. When the maintenance man inspected the bathroom stall that had been used by Melissa only moments before, he was shocked to find the walls and floor covered in blood. He was even more stunned to discover a newborn baby wrapped in a plastic bag in the restroom garbage bin.

Medical emergency personnel were immediately summoned to the birth scene and worked aggressively to resuscitate the newborn. The infant was rushed to the Bayshore Community Hospital in Holmdel Township for additional lifesaving measures. However, despite heroic efforts, physicians were unable to revive Melissa Drexler's baby.

Even before the end of the senior prom, Melissa was identified as the mother of the abandoned infant. Other students had witnessed her unusual behavior in the restroom, and the discovery of blood and the body of the baby led directly to her. When first questioned about the incident, she refused to disclose any details to investigators; however, she readily admitted that she had given birth to the infant found in the trash container. After a brief interview with law enforcement officials, Melissa was taken to the same hospital that had admitted her baby; she was suffering from minor complications from the birthing process. There the placenta was removed; she was given a thorough medical examination and released to her parents. No charges were filed against Drexler at the time.

Surprisingly, most of the other students at the senior prom seemed to be completely unaware of the events that had transpired in their midst that evening. The senior class president and the high school principal both confirmed that the students at the dance knew little, if any, of what had occurred in the banquet hall restroom. Apparently talk of the birth and death of a newborn during the prom stirred little interest at the time and was considered by most of the attendees to be more rumor than fact. According to the senior class president, "There was talk about someone who miscarried in the bathroom or lost their baby or something, but no one really knew what they were talking about. With stories that go from person to person, you never know what the truth is."[27] However, within twenty-four hours everyone in Lacey Township would know the name of Melissa Drexler, as would most of the nation, in what proved to be a sensational story that captured enduring and horrifying headlines.

Like so many pregnant teenagers, Melissa Drexler was able to hide her pregnancy from everyone around her. During her conversations with investigators and medical personnel on the night of the prom, the adolescent repeatedly emphasized that no one, including her family, had been aware of her pregnancy. To the officials in the area, this idea seemed hard to accept. The Monmouth County prosecutor, John Kaye, reacted with particular skepticism to Melissa's statements to authorities: "It always is surprising to me that somebody can carry a baby to term and people don't know it. I've spoken to people in situations like that who were convincingly unaware."[28]

However, Melissa's friends were sincere and unanimous in their surprise at learning that their classmate had been pregnant. The question that now burned in the minds of authorities and residents of the township was a painful one that could not be avoided: had this quiet, seemingly ideal teenager murdered her own infant in an inexplicable act of violence, or had the baby actually been stillborn?

Investigators combed the Garden Manor banquet hall restroom and surrounding areas for evidence of any crime. The bathroom scene was a grotesque display of blood, and several individuals had visited the facilities after Melissa Drexler left the area, making the collection of forensic evidence problematic. However, some items were located and collected. Still, investigating officers were unable to locate any instrument that may have been used to sever the infant's umbilical cord— a piece of evidence that investigators believed could prove significant in their investigation.

Less than a week after the prom, preliminary autopsy details were released in the death of "Baby Boy Drexler." The autopsy, which was performed by Dr. Jay A. Peacock, the first assistant medical examiner for the county, showed that the infant had been alive during the birthing process and had not died of any obvious wounds or trauma. The full details that a complete autopsy could provide were not yet available; however, based on the preliminary medical findings, a final report seemed critical to any case that might be brought against Melissa Drexler. A detailed and careful autopsy would determine whether the infant had survived birth or was stillborn. In order for authorities to bring a charge of murder against the young mother, the infant had to have been born alive. The key issue in cases such as these, from a legal standpoint, is whether or not the infant had been capable of living independently of his or her mother. For the next few weeks, the Drexler family, the residents of Lacey Township, local officials and authorities, and many citizens across the nation waited anxiously for the final medical report.

In the case of Melissa Drexler's baby, at least one factor complicated and delayed the final medical findings. One of the determining issues in a decision about the viability of a newborn is the presence of oxygen and other gases in the lungs. In the case of the Drexler baby, one of the results of the heroic but unsuccessful resuscitation efforts on the night of June 6 was that oxygen and carbon dioxide had been artificially introduced into the infant's lungs, thereby making a definitive autopsy result more complex, if not impossible. By the third week in June, when the final results of the autopsy were expected, some officials and medical experts were beginning to send signals to the press that a final conclusion might be out of reach. Isidore Mihalakis, the Warren County medical examiner, expressed these concerns most clearly to local reporters:

I'm not sure they'll ever be able to prove whether the baby breathed [on his own]. Even that test [an examination to determine if the infant's lungs contained oxygen and carbon dioxide] may not clear up the question of whether the air in the baby's lungs got there from his own breathing or from the mouth of a rescue worker.[29]

The Drexler family had to wait for the final results of the autopsy to learn something of Melissa's fate. During those weeks the family refused to discuss the birth or death of the newborn, despite intense pressure from dozens of reporters who constantly besieged the Drexler home. However, fearing the worst, the Drexlers engaged an attorney from Ocean County, Steven Secare, to represent their daughter.

Two weeks after the tragic events at the senior prom, Melissa was still in seclusion at her parents' home, reportedly grief stricken. Neither Melissa nor her boyfriend were able to discuss the death of their baby, and the young mother was much too upset and embarrassed to attend her own high school graduation ceremonies. According to one of Melissa's and John's closest friends, it still seemed impossible that the adolescent could have harmed her baby in any way: "Melissa could never hurt anyone, we all know that. And we all know the autopsy results are going to come back and show that."[30]

The couple's friend also again confirmed that John Lewis had been completely unaware of Melissa's pregnancy until she gave birth on June 6. However, by this time that claim had been thrown into question by an interview that took place on June 11, less than a week after the tragedy. On that day, an alleged friend of Drexler's confidentially told a reporter for the *Asbury Park Press* that the young woman had admitted to her that she was pregnant but had believed that her baby was not due for another three weeks.

On June 24, 1997, the long-awaited results of Baby Boy Drexler's autopsy were released. The report was stunning and tragic for the Drexler family: the infant had either been strangled or had died from suffocation after being placed in the plastic bag and abandoned in the trash receptacle. According to a statement made by John Kaye after he read the medical examiner's report, there was no question that the newborn had been murdered.

Based on the results of the autopsy, Melissa Drexler was immediately charged with two felonies: murder and endangering a child. The combined charges could carry a maximum sentence of the death penalty or, alternatively, life in prison. That same day the teenager voluntarily surrendered to authorities and entered an initial plea of innocent to the charges against her. Throughout her hearing Drexler appeared distraught and frightened, her voice barely audible to those in the courtroom. At the end of the hearing Superior Court Judge John Ricciardi set Drexler's bail at $50,000. The amount was quickly posted, and Melissa was allowed to return to her family's home. Three months later, on September 17, Drexler was formally indicted for murder by a grand jury in Freehold, New Jersey. However, she remained free on the original bail; prosecutor Kaye told reporters that he would not seek the death penalty, "due to her age, her lack of [a] criminal record, and her emotional state."[31] On August 20, 1998, Melissa pleaded guilty to a reduced charge of aggravated manslaughter. Prosecutors asked that she be sentenced to 15 years in prison; she could be eligible for parole in under three years.

On the day the final autopsy results were released, Kaye had held a news conference in Freehold, where he disclosed some of the previously unknown details of Baby Drexler's apparent murder. According to Kaye's statements, Drexler probably used the sharp edge of a sanitary-napkin dispenser to cut the infant's umbilical cord before dumping the boy in a plastic bag that she had discovered in the bathroom stall. The autopsy report clearly showed that air existed in the baby's intestines, proving that he had been able to breathe on his own after birth. The official cause of death was listed as "asphyxia due to manual strangulation and obstruction of the external airway or orifices," although the prosecutor later conceded that the infant could have suffocated from being wrapped in the plastic bag used by Drexler to dispose of the newborn.[32]

Kaye also disclosed that Drexler had said to a girlfriend who came into the restroom looking for her while she was giving birth, "Go tell the boys we'll be right out," indicating that she was aware of her environment and apparently in control of the situation. She had then cleaned herself, put her black prom dress back on, and returned to the dance floor, leaving the restroom stall covered with blood.[33] During the course of the news conference, Kaye noted that Drexler had apparently been successful in completely hiding her pregnancy from her family and friends, although he could not explain how such a secret could have been maintained by the teenager.

It was clear from the prosecutor's press conference that his office believed it had a very strong case against the Lacey Township teenager. However, as is true with most cases of adolescents who murder their newborns, there was controversy surrounding the question of motive. It was left to Melissa's attorney to comment on his client's perspective on the tragic situation.

When Steven Secare was asked by reporters about Melissa's state of mind surrounding the events of June 6, 1997, he answered with a theme common in cases of neonaticide committed by teenagers: "She understands what the charges are against her and their severity. [However,] I don't think she has total comprehension of everything that's happening to her. I don't think anyone could."[34] He then emphasized that Melissa was in complete denial about her pregnancy and did not believe that she had committed murder.

Once again, as in the case of Amy Grossberg and so many other teenage mothers, the emotional forces of shame, fear, and denial rose to the forefront of the issue of neonaticide. Looking back on the facts of this case, it seems likely that the teenager was completely overwhelmed by her pregnancy and ultimately unable to find an alternative to murder. If this was the situation, the moral aspects of her actions would certainly have been difficult ones for the judge responsible for the question of punishment.

GLIMPSES OF A SECRET CRIME

The stunning case of Melissa Drexler prompted reporters covering the story to ask the prosecutor, John Kaye, about other cases of neonaticide that had occurred in this quiet, seemingly crime-free community. In part, the question was prompted by members of the press who, in their background research into neonaticide, had become aware that plea-bargaining was quite common in such crimes. Young women, especially teenagers, who were initially charged with murder in such cases were usually allowed to plead guilty to a lesser charge before trial. Because of the sensationalism of the Drexler case, the local press and residents were understandably curious about what the teenager's future might hold. There was also a driving interest within this close-knit community to come to some understanding of a crime that is quite often incomprehensible.

The residents were understandably surprised to learn that ten such crimes had been investigated in their area in the past decade.[35] In the majority of these cases, the perpetrator had eventually pleaded guilty to a lesser charge than that originally filed by prosecutors. In one instance, the perpetrator was never identified.

Included in this small but representative cross-section of neonaticide were these cases:

- In 1994, Karen Ann Dobrzelecki, a nineteen-year-old from Berkeley Township, had given birth to a son, alone and unassisted, in her own home. After the delivery the adolescent had placed her newborn in a plastic garbage bag and concealed the baby in her closet. Four days later, the infant's body was discovered. In the Dobrzelecki case, which had several points in common with the Melissa Drexler case, prosecutors had accepted a guilty plea to aggravated manslaughter instead of to the original charge of murder.

- A twenty-six-year-old woman, Doris Weigand, of Neptune, New Jersey, had been the perpetrator of an especially gruesome murder that had made national headlines a decade before the Drexler case. On March 29, 1987, she self-delivered her infant while sitting in a bathtub filled with water. After giving birth underwater, she retrieved the infant, put him in a towel, and then strangled him to death with his umbilical cord. Weigand then disposed of the body in a garbage container and informed police that she had had a miscarriage. The woman was initially charged with murder but later pleaded guilty to aggravated manslaughter. Weigand had been sentenced to prison for twenty years.

- An eighteen-year-old Trinton Falls teenager, Suzanne Price, had been able to hide her pregnancy from her family and friends until she gave birth, alone, in her own bathroom, on March 19, 1990. Immediately after his birth Price had stabbed the infant to death with a pair of scissors. She was subsequently arrested and charged with murder. However, Price had insisted that she had no memory of the crime or even of the birth of her son. She had eventually pleaded guilty to aggravated manslaughter and was sentenced to ten years in prison.

- A seventeen-year-old adolescent from Asbury Park had given birth to a baby girl in her own bathroom in December 1991. Although details of the case were not made public because of the age of the perpetrator, an assistant prosecutor for the county had confirmed that the newborn was drowned in the toilet. The juvenile was initially charged with aggravated manslaughter and later pleaded guilty to a reduced charge of manslaughter. She had been sentenced to a year of probation and mandated family counseling; the court records in the case were sealed.

- On April 18, 1992, a newborn baby girl had been found on a beach in Sea Girt, New Jersey. The body had been wrapped in a plastic garbage bag. When autopsied, the infant's remains exhibited evidence of cocaine; it was determined that she had died of asphyxia and exposure. The mother of the newborn was never found, and no charges were ever filed in the case.

DISSOCIATIVE DISORDERS—A COMMON THREAD?

Discussing the Melissa Drexler case with local reporters, Dr. Charles D. Katz, a pediatric psychologist at Monmouth Medical Center, pointed out the possibility that the adolescent may have been suffering from a severe dissociative disorder at the time she murdered her newborn.[36] If so, the effects of this disorder may have left Drexler so anxious and afraid that she was able to completely detach herself emotionally from her gruesome actions of June 6, 1997. This motivational argument is a common theme in many cases of neonaticide committed by adolescents and young women; in fact, it is central to the defense strategy for many of these teenagers. It may help to explain the overwhelming impact of shame, fear, and guilt that so often accompanies a teenage pregnancy that ends in violence.

At the end of the nineteenth century, the renowned psychologist and physician Pierre Janet introduced the term "dissociation" into the medical literature. The French healer noticed that certain systems of ideas normally held in a unified fashion in consciousness can be split off from the fundamental personality and exist wholly outside the individual's awareness. This important discovery led to the modern concept of dissociative disorders, which include three major categories: (1) *multiple personality disorder*, (2) *psychogenic fugue* (known more recently as "dissociative fugue"), and (3) *psychogenic amnesia* (known more recently as "dissociative amnesia").

Of these three dissociative disorders, multiple personality disorder is widely known in this nation because of a variety of best-selling books and media presentations about the topic. However, it is an extremely rare disorder, one that is very difficult to identify accurately, diagnose, and treat. Even though recognition of its presence is often delayed until adolescence or young adulthood, the roots of multiple personality disorder arise in childhood. It is frequently linked to a childhood filled with abuse, trauma, and neglect. In the vast majority of cases of neonaticide, the possibility that the perpetrator is suffering from multiple personality disorder is not a significant consideration.

Psychogenic (or dissociative) fugue, is also a rare disorder, although not as rare as multiple personality disorder. It is most often characterized by the victim suddenly and unconsciously abandoning his or her current lifestyle and location in favor of a new identity and lifestyle.[37] These symptoms include:

- Sudden and unexpected travel away from home or workplace, with inability to recall the past.
- Confusion about personal identity or the assumption of a new identity.
- The onset of the disorder is not due to the effects of a medical condition or ingestion of substances.
- Significant impairment in social, occupational, or other important areas of functioning.

Often this disorder is linked to highly stressful or traumatic events in the victim's life. When the fugue state occurs, its onset is extremely rapid; when it passes, the fugue state can leave the victim with little or no memory of intervening events or actions. However, in the dissociative state the sufferer may be able to function in society, although this is certainly not always the case. In defense of perpetrators of neonaticide legal arguments have been offered that rely on the traumatizing impact of an unwanted pregnancy as the possible catalyst of a psychogenic fugue condition.

The third category of dissociative disorders, psychogenic (or dissociative) amnesia, is more common than either multiple personality disorder or psychogenic fugue. The disorder is characterized by a sudden inability to recall personal information or events. The amnesia state can be mild or profound, depending on the causal factors and the victim. In extreme cases, victims are completely disoriented, extremely confused, and profoundly perplexed. However, they may still be able to carry out difficult or trying tasks. The victim does not assume a false or new identity with this disorder. Its diagnostic criteria are:[38]

- Episodes of inability to recall important information, usually of a traumatic or stressful nature.
- The disturbance is not caused by a medical condition or the ingestion of substances.

• Significant impairment in social, occupational, or other important areas of functioning.

Psychogenic amnesia, like psychogenic fugue, is linked to personal trauma or crisis, particularly if the victim has been threatened with bodily harm or death. As in the case of psychogenic fugue, this disorder has formed the basis for the explanation of some cases of neonaticide.

Dissociative disorders are not completely understood by behaviorists, psychologists, and psychiatrists. They occur with a broad spectrum of variations, in a wide range of individuals. Effects can range from very debilitating, as in the case of multiple personality disorder, to momentary and extreme outbursts of inexplicable behavior. In this sense, much of what we have come to learn about neonaticide, particularly when it is committed by an adolescent, seems to correlate to dissociative disorders. Certainly, the argument can be made that a pregnant teenager often fears for her physical safety, is terrified of what others (particularly her parents and other adults) will think of her, and is frequently overwhelmed by guilt and shame. For some adolescents, pregnancy may represent an extremely traumatizing event that triggers intense denial and fear. In this sense, pregnancy may also produce a dissociative state that, for a few teenagers, leads to murder.

A HORRIBLE CRIME WITH MANY VICTIMS

It is indisputable that neonaticide is among the most gruesome and unforgivable of crimes. Not only does the miraculous innocence of birth seem to most of us something to be held sacrosanct and inviolable, but the complete helplessness and physical dependence of these victims adds a particular and unique horror to this crime. Because we are human, the overwhelming majority of us value life beyond all else. We not only strive to perfect our own lives but also instill in our children a regard for life that, we hope, is unshakable and un-questionable. Most precious to us are the infants—living representations of the essential meaning and joy of life itself. When one of these tiny victims is struck down, we are all saddened and diminished.

Moreover, neonaticide is often an act of deeply personal and extreme violence. Whether by suffocation, strangulation, or other direct force, when his or her own mother murders a newborn in such a personal way we are outraged. How can these young mothers commit such an unspeakable act, and apparently do so without conscience? How can this happen in what we have come to believe is a highly civilized and caring society? Especially, how can such "good kids" commit such incredible acts of violence?

Our outraged, angry reaction to such crimes is understandable. If we did not react in this way it would be questionable whether we had that unique spark of humanity that separates us from the other species. However, despite the horrors of neonaticide, we must look beyond the obvious victim: when this crime is committed, there are many victims. When an adolescent murders her newborn, she is destroying more than a single life—she is also striking out against herself, her family, her future, and ours. There are many victims in every incident of neonaticide, and some of them are often the subject of our outrage and anger rather than our compassion. Nonetheless, they too are victims.

When an adolescent with an unquestioned background of honesty, integrity, and kindness suddenly lashes out in this most horrific way, our assumption is that she is in fact nothing more than a "bad kid." This kind of abandonment of the perpetrator, which often occurs even in those who have known her all her life, is typical and somewhat understandable. However, it is fundamentally wrong. Worse, such an unthinking reaction may close our minds to the possibilities of doing more about such a gruesome crime than insisting on the worst form of punishment the law allows.

This is not to advocate that those who commit neonaticide should simply be forgiven for their awful crimes and allowed to walk away from their cruel deeds unpunished. That would obviously be ludicrous and unthinkable. However, when many of these adolescents murder their newborns, they do not suddenly become bad kids; they are not instantly and inexplicably transformed into the kind of sociopath who would commit such a brutal crime merely for the pleasure of the act. These are still good kids, who for reasons we are only now beginning to understand commit the most atrocious crimes. When this kind of violence occurs, as it does all too often in America, we must not only work to understand the perpetrator and her history, we must also look deeply into ourselves and judge to what extent, if any, we have indirectly contributed to the murder of a newborn by an unwillingness to examine the totality of the crime.

NOTES

1. James W. Prado and Jason Method, "Denial of Pregnancy Called Common among Teens," *Asbury Park* (New Jersey) *Press* (Internet Edition), 10 June 1997.

2. Charles Patrick Ewing. *Kids Who Kill* (New York: Avon Books, 1990), 133.

3. Ibid., 133.

4. Ibid., 134.

5. American Broadcasting Company, Inc., *Good Morning America* (television program), aired 7 July 1997.

6. Pat Wiedenkeller, "Pregnancy, Denial, Tragedy," *Newsday* (Internet Edition), 21 November 1996.

7. Ibid.

8. Ibid.

9. Andrew Smith, "Conviction Stands in Baby Death: Mom's Prison Term to Start," *Newsday* (Internet Edition), 22 November 1996.

10. Elizabeth Gleick, "Three Kids, One Death," *Time* (Internet Edition) 128, no. 25 (2 December 1996).

11. Steve Wick, Karen Anderson, Chau Lam, and Rose

Schaer, "Sweethearts Now Suspects," *Newsday* (Internet Edition), 19 November 1996.

12. Mary Mostert, "College Freshmen from Affluent Homes Kill Their Baby," *Monthly Monitor* (Internet Edition), 19 November 1996.

13. Ibid.

14. Wick, et al.

15. Ibid.

16. Ibid.

17. "Teen Surrenders in Baby's Death," *San Francisco Chronicle* (Internet Edition), 21 November 1996.

18. "Trash-Bin Baby Born Alive, Autopsy Shows," *San Francisco Examiner* (Internet Edition), Nation Headlines, 22 November 1996.

19. "Accused Baby-Killers Offer Hint of Defense," *Houston Chronicle* (Internet Edition), 17 December 1996.

20. "New Jersey Teen Says She Did Not Kill Her Baby," *Reuters Limited* (Internet Edition), 6 June 1997.

21. Ibid.

22. Ibid.

23. Robin Topping, "Around the Island/Crime and the Courts," *Newsday* (Internet Edition), 30 July 1997.

24. Cori Anne Natoli, "Quiet Drexlers in Eye of News Storm," *Home News and Tribune,* published in the *Asbury Park* (New Jersey) *Press* (Internet Edition), 22 June 1997.

25. Ibid.

26. Margaret Carlson, "Prom Nightmare: A Dead Baby in the Wastebasket, a Debate Gone Awry," *Time* (Internet Edition), 129, no. 25 (21 June 1997).

27. Lisa Fried and Allison Garvey, "Baby's Autopsy Results Awaited," *Asbury Park* (New Jersey) *Press* (Internet Edition), 16 June 1997.

28. Ibid.

29. Lisa Fried, "Coroner Holds Key in Prom Birth Case," *Home News and Tribune,* published in the *Asbury Park* (New Jersey) *Press* (Internet Edition), 23 June 1997.

30. Bob Mura and Allison Garvey, "Prom Mom Grief-Stricken, Friend Reveals," *Home News and Tribune,* published in the *Asbury Park* (New Jersey) *Press* (Internet Edition), 20 June 1997.

31. "Grand Jury Charges U.S. Girl with Killing Baby," *Reuters News Service* (Internet Edition), 17 September 1997.

32. "New Jersey Teen Pleads Innocent in Death of Newborn Boy at Prom," *Houston Chronicle News Services* (Internet Edition), 24 June 1997.

33. Ibid.

34. Bob Mura and Cori Anne Natoli, "Baby Born at Senior Prom Laid to Rest," *Home News and Tribune,* published in the *Asbury Park* (New Jersey) *Press* (Internet Edition), 29 June 1997.

35. Elaine Silvestrini and Patricia A. Miller, "In Other Cases, Plea to Lesser Charge Has Been the Rule," *Home News and Tribune,* published in the *Asbury Park* (New Jersey) *Press* (Internet Edition), 25 June 1997.

36. Regina McEnery, "Air in Baby's Intestines A Sign That He Lived," *Home News and Tribune,* published in the *Asbury Park* (New Jersey) *Press* (Internet Edition), 25 June 1997.

37. American Psychiatric Association, *Diagnostic and Statistical Manual of Mental Disorders,* 4th ed. (1994), 484.

38. Ibid., 481.

3

RAGE AND RETRIBUTION

I know of no more disagreeable situation than to be left feeling generally angry without anybody in particular to be angry at.

Frank Moore Colby
The Colby Essays, Vol. 1

In 1955, James Dean riveted the consciousness of parents and adolescents across this nation with his disturbing and moving performance in the acclaimed Nicholas Ray movie *Rebel Without a Cause.* The role Dean played in this classic film was that of Jim Stark, a troubled and displaced teenager who found himself in a series of irresolvable conflicts with the middle-class values of his parents and the older generation that surrounded him. Dean vividly brought to life the emerging, powerful frustrations and anger that confronted this otherwise typical high school teenager throughout his short, chaotic life—a growing, inevitable rage that inexorably impelled Stark toward his own destruction.

Among the many poignant aspects of this movie was the strong emotional conflict that existed between Stark's angry character and the inability of his parents to recognize the intense pain and misdirection in their own child's life. In the end, the adult world that surrounded and closed in on Jim Stark was thrown into confusion and a sense of helpless resignation by the teenager's escalating frustration and rage. They could only view Jim Stark's self-destructive behavior as utterly pointless and incomprehensibly catastrophic—not as something understandable in their own lives. Only Stark's teenage companions could muster a true understanding of the anger that flowed so vehemently within the heart of this rebel without a cause. They knew that Stark, at root, was a sensitive and caring person but one who, like themselves, had been set adrift in a seemingly alien and hostile world. In this classic screen drama, as in life, it was the angry adolescent's friends who best understood Jim Stark's fierce pain, because they also felt it so profoundly.

On September 30, 1955, James Dean was tragically killed in an automobile accident, leaving behind a vision of teenage anger and rebellion that remains with us today. What Dean brought to the art of cinema was not merely an obvious talent for his role but a compelling insight into the deep emotional turmoil of adolescence. In this sense, Dean left us an enduring legacy that continues to be valid more than forty years after the actor's death.

Today, as when *Rebel Without a Cause* was playing in movie theatres throughout this country, a fundamental understanding of the seemingly senseless violence of our children still eludes us. James Dean created a vivid portrayal of teenage isolation and rage, but his work provided us no certain answers. We still search for that illusive emotional understanding of the seething anger that seems to assail so many of our children. Still, Dean's role in this movie bequeathed to us a clear vision of the obvious emotional divide that often exists between adolescents and adults. Perhaps this emotional legacy was one of the most poignant (and most often overlooked) points of this compelling production.

However, the cinema is rarely a perfect reflection of life—nor is it usually intended to be so. When an adolescent rages out of control, he *can* become a ruthless, lethal murderer of the most brutal type. His actions are often inexplicable, unreasonable, and beyond the comprehension of most adults. This is frequently the reality with which we, as parents, must grapple when we examine the violent crimes of our children. Moreover, our concern is most deep and profound when the rage within an adolescent is directed against the youngster's parents—when the violence becomes parricide. This kind of horrifying crime profoundly chills our hearts and leaves us deeply hurt and confused. Even though parricide is a relatively rare crime in our society, it remains one of the most disturbing and frightening forms of teenage violence we can imagine.

In many instances, the effects of adolescent rage are clearly self-directed and self-destructive. However, in some cases a teenager does not turn his rage inward, like Jim Stark, but strikes against those whom he truly loves but who also symbolize the isolation and alienation that he experiences so strongly. In a few cases, the adolescent lashes out in a moment of uncontrolled passion and violence that cannot be recaptured. Rare as these moments are, they do occur in this country, and they do so across all socioeconomic barriers.

When these crimes against the family are committed, they are fueled by a kind of rage that is incomprehensible to most adults. The actions of these teenagers are abhorrently violent in their outcome and usually completely foreign to all adults who knew the perpetrator. However, the perpetrator's peers often instinctively understand this kind of extraordinary violence, even though they will agree that the crime itself was abhorrent. The most shocking fact about parricide is that this terrifying crime is frequently committed by a previously nonviolent adolescent—a person who has given little or no warning of the extraordinary explosion that was forthcoming.

For example, in February 1996 a fourteen-year-old California teenager chased his mother around the family home with a handgun and finally shot her to death, after arguing with her over what should have been a trivial family matter. This adolescent murderer had no criminal record and no history of violence before his outrageous outburst. He had been by all accounts a completely nonviolent individual, exceptionally close to his family.

Two weeks later, a fifteen-year-old Nevada teenager who was visiting his grandparents' home bludgeoned five members of his family to death: his mother, father, both grandparents, and his ten-year-old sister. Like the California teenager, he was raging with anger at his family but had no prior history of criminality or violence. However, unlike the California case, this youngster did have a history of angry verbal confrontations with his father. Was this sufficient reason for murder? Certainly, to the victims, murder would not have seemed possible.

What these two teenage killers shared in common was the sudden, catastrophic upwelling of an uncontrollable rage, an upwelling that resulted in acts of extreme and gruesome violence against their own families. However, in neither case could the perpetrators afterward provide what most adults would recognize as an understandable motive for murder. Like most cases of parricide, the crimes of these adolescents seem extraordinary and inexplicable in relation to what, as adults, we would perceive as anything like a reasonable reaction to parental control.

What we must ask about this kind of violence is troublesome and, perhaps, unanswerable. However, it is fundamental, if we are to make inroads against this kind of crime in the future. *Where* did this compelling force of rage begin in our children? How did it come to be there, and why is it such an overwhelming situation for a few teenagers? What, if anything, can be done to avoid a heinous outcome?

If we are to be the best parents to our children, we cannot simply put this issue aside and hope for a nonviolent future. We must recognize that there are no simple answers to any questions surrounding why otherwise good kids suddenly resort to murder. Despite our current lack of clear answers, we must press forward to come to some understanding of why our children kill in such a mindless, brutal fashion. In the final analysis, we cannot afford to make the same mistakes as Jim Stark's parents and resign ourselves to the sense of helplessness that naturally accompanies the inexplicable violence of our sons and daughters. James Dean's artistry made it clear that such mistakes are enormous in their impact, even if they are quite understandable.

THAT FAMILIAR, FRIGHTENING FEELING

On October 1, 1997, a sixteen-year-old high school sophomore brutally murdered three individuals and wounded another seven, reportedly because he was in an uncontrollable rage. Before leaving for school that morning, Luke Woodham of Pearl, Mississippi, stabbed his mother to death with a butcher knife, apparently because he was distraught over a breakup with his girlfriend. After killing his mother Woodham went to his high school, armed with a rifle hidden beneath his trench coat. There he opened fire on his former girlfriend and other students in the immediate area, killing two outright and wounding seven others. Trying to escape from the scene in his mother's car, the teenager was rammed by a vehicle driven by

Snapshot Profile of Luke Woodham

A sixteen-year-old high school student, who had no history of violence or criminal activities. Angry because he had just broken up with his girlfriend, Woodham stabbed his mother to death and then went to his high school with a concealed rifle. At the school the teenager shot and killed his former girlfriend, another student, and wounded seven others in a shooting spree that was at least partially random in nature. His stated motive for the rampage was that he was angry at the way he had been treated by others. After Woodham's arrest, officials in the area began an investigation into an alleged ring of teenagers who had apparently conspired among themselves to commit murder. However, some charges were dropped and no case has yet been brought to court. One can only wonder if this kind of reaction was driven by the shock and fear brought about by Luke Woodham's outrageous attack on his classmates.

a school employee and taken into custody. Just prior to the shooting spree Woodham had handed a handwritten note to a classmate that outlined his motive for the rampage: "I am not insane. I am angry."[1]

When adolescents like Luke Woodham try to describe the inexplicable forces of anger and rage that sometimes overwhelm them, they are almost always at a loss to characterize precisely the genesis of such strong emotions. Nonetheless, they can usually describe in detail the extreme emotional state itself—the frightening, all-encompassing feeling that accompanies their rage, even when it seems to arise from nowhere. Moreover, most teenagers who experience these overpowering waves of anger are not only stunned at its sudden onslaught but also frightened by its implications.

One adolescent of seventeen, describing the inexplicable, overpowering anger he felt against his mother, said, "You get this feeling of pure rage coming somewhere from inside of you. It's like being drunk . . . drunk with rage. Things can happen before anyone can stop it. It's scary."[2] Another youngster, sixteen years old, described the overwhelming emotion that led to his physical violence against his mother: "When I get mad, things are just a blur. I guess I pushed her into the wall or something. She was just bugging me, about my friends and stuff. I just kinda went off."[3]

As frightening as these two examples are, neither adolescent involved in them murdered a parent. In the end, both teenagers were able to pass through their periods of rage with the help of understanding parents, and in one case, the committed assistance of a counselor. It was only years later, when these individuals looked back on those moments of uncontrolled anger, that both youngsters realized the extreme danger of their pitched emotions. When they did so, they were filled with a fear of what might have occurred and were grateful that they did not act more fully on their feelings of rage. Sadly, some adolescents do not manage to regain emotional control before it is lost with devastating and life-destroying consequences.

A LOSS OF CONTROL

An obvious concern of parents, which arises naturally from reports of the crime of parricide, is how to distinguish between routine or normal adolescent anger and the kind of seething, uncontrollable rage that can lead to murder. In truth, there is no way to make such a distinction with absolute reliability. However, experts in adolescent behavior tend to agree on general guidelines that can help to distinguish routine adolescent anger from a potentially murderous rage:

Yelling, pouting, moodiness, persistent complaining, slamming doors and ripping up things, while not desirable, are behaviors usually within normal limits of teenage anger. But substantial destruction of property or leaving the home for hours is not OK, and any threat of bodily harm to themselves or others should be taken very seriously.[4]

Clearly, this kind of advice is very broad, and its implications, if taken at face value, can be deceiving. However, studies of violent crimes committed by adolescents against their parents indicate that there is sometimes a noticeable escalation in aggressive behavior that precedes an extremely violent outburst. The difficulty is that, in some cases, this escalation of behavior seems to take place very abruptly and without expectation or recognition on the part of the teenager's parents. Possible signs are:[5]

- Abruptly abandoning old friends for new ones
- An unwillingness to allow parents to meet new friends
- A drop in grades at school or abandonment of interest in school
- Rapid change in moods or unusually severe mood swings
- Increasing defiance of regulations
- Increasing conflict with authority figures

- Increasing secretiveness
- Profound laziness or disinterest in normal activities
- Withdrawal from family gatherings and activities
- Abrupt and negative changes in physical appearance or hygiene
- Avoidance of home, especially by persistently staying out late at night
- Money, alcohol, or prescription drugs missing from the home

In general, individuals familiar with adolescent behavior usually advise parents and other adults to be observant for significant or abrupt changes in a teenager's behavior patterns. Such changes can be a sign that the adolescent is undergoing stressful life experiences and could benefit from positive, caring intervention from a trusted adult. As is so often at the core of successful and positive human interaction, open and honest communication is the key to avoiding potential aggression.

It is important to realize that even if an adolescent exhibits one or more of the general warning signs that may indicate growing anger, it is not necessarily an assurance that he or she is approaching an out-of-control situation that can lead to violence or murder. At best, all we can say is that these signs are sometimes associated with teenagers who are on the path to uncontrollable anger, rage, and, in a few instances, physical violence. Unfortunately, in a number of cases the ultimate expression of rage and violence is directed at those who are closest to the angry and uncontrolled adolescent—his or her parents.

ATTACKING THE FAMILY

It is important to realize that despite the sensational headlines that always seem to accompany parricide, this is not a major category of crime in the United States. Of all juveniles who commit murder each year in this country, only about 8 percent of them murder one or more of their parents. However, despite the relative rarity of this kind of violence, there is a disturbing similarity among the profiles of teenagers who do commit parental murder.

Typically, the adolescent who murders a parent is a son rather than a daughter. He is most often Caucasian and middle class, usually with above-average intelligence. Also, the perpetrator typically has no criminal record and no history of significant violence in his background, and he may come from a single-parent household. Emotionally, he may exhibit some difficulties in school, an emerging pattern of argumentative behavior with others, and possibly an unresolved problem with alcohol or drugs. It is also possible that one or more of his parents was a substance abuser or that the adolescent was the victim of parental sexual or physical abuse in his early childhood.

In some cases, the adolescent who murders a parent has witnessed significant family violence as a child and therefore developed a strong view that such violence is an acceptable form of behavior. However, this crime also happens in families with no history of violence between its members. At best, the argument can be made that an adolescent who has witnessed prolonged and severe violence within the family environment may be more likely to use violence against others in many situations. This is a generally accepted model of violent behavior, but it certainly does not apply exclusively to those teenagers who commit parricide.

Finally, in a few instances, there may be a long-term, debilitating psychological disorder at the root of an adolescent's violent outburst, although this is clearly not the case in the majority of crimes of parricide.[6] The possible role of short-term, transient psychological disorders in many cases of teenage parricide remains a contested issue among law enforcement personnel, the legal system, and behaviorists.

As there are certain background and behavioral similarities among many teenagers who murder their parents, there is also a discernable pattern that describes the circumstances and method of their crimes. For example, when adolescents turn against one or both parents in any kind of physically violent way, more than half do so as the direct result of a family-related argument. This statistic remains valid when the teenager's physical aggression turns to murder. Also, nearly two-thirds of the perpetrators of parricide use a firearm to commit their crime, and usually this weapon belongs to another member of the family.[7]

Nonetheless, however interesting and helpful to an understanding of this crime, the profile of children who murder a parent does not shed much light on the question of motivation. Moreover, as the case histories that follow will show, such a profile often proves to be inaccurate. In the final analysis, we are able to recognize only a vague outline of the profile of an adolescent murderer who lashes out against family members. We often find ourselves stunned by the crime of parricide and more uncertain about the crime, because each latest perpetrator overturns our then-current knowledge and assumptions.

In fact, the typical perpetrator of parricide does not come close to satisfying the average American's assumptions about most killers. This is especially true when the issue of motivation is considered. Certainly, these raging, violent adolescents are rarely psychopathic murderers, although they occasionally murder for money, freedom, or possessions. However, they are not career criminals in the strict definition of the term. In fact, these young killers are often described by those who knew them as nonviolent, pleasant, and stable individuals. As we often read in the press and see on television, adolescents who have just brutally murdered a parent are regularly described with positive and sometimes even glowing terms—phrases that lead us to believe that they could have been nothing but upstanding, ideal individuals. And in fact, perpetrators of parricide are often just that.

In that secret moment of terminal rage, these otherwise impeccable teenagers can be mysteriously and inexplicably transformed into the most brutal killers. Worse, none of us seem to understand why this transformation happens or what it means. Transfixed by what we find in the media, we can only feel the pain and shock of the victims, and perhaps a sense of gratitude that we were spared such a horror in our own lives.

Although psychologists, behaviorists, and experts in adolescent behavior have offered a variety of explanations for adolescent rage, there is little consensus about the issue, and even less hard information that can be of practical value. In the end, we are left with only the sad case histories of teenagers who strike out against their parents, family members, or close friends, to help illuminate what is certainly one of the darkest and most confusing categories of violent crimes.

"The Most Loving Family I've Ever Seen"

Yorba Linda is an unusually relaxed, placid community, located less than an hour's drive from the frenetic metropolis of Los Angeles. Although known to many Americans as the home of the Richard Nixon Presidential Library, this town has managed to retain an appealing and traditional mid-American size and personality. It is still considered one of the safest, most comfortable communities in this otherwise bustling, overpopulated part of California. Life in this place has an easy, routine pace that is reflected in well-maintained, sometimes stately, homes and shady, charming streets. In 1996, the mayor of Yorba Linda, John M. Gullixson, described his town in a conventional way that reflected the inherent pride and satisfaction of its citizens: "This is the kind of community where everybody knows each other."[8] In most ways, the citizenry of Yorba Linda has always felt very much at home and safe in the traditional, protected, family-oriented environment.

With a population of fifty-seven thousand, Yorba Linda is justifiably proud of its exceptionally low crime rate, especially when compared to the unchecked violence that plagues much of the metropolitan Los Angeles area to the south. In 1995, the city experienced no homicides and very little general crime. However, in 1996 this idyllic community experienced one of the most inexplicable and disturbing murders in its long history when a fourteen-year-old shot and killed his mother over an incredibly insignificant family dispute.

Phillip Connolly, a fire captain with the Orange County Fire Authority, and his wife, Cindy, lived with their two children on a tree-lined cul-de-sac in an established and comfortable area of town. By all accounts the Connolly family was happy and well regarded by all who knew them. This was particularly true of Cindy, who, at the age of forty-two worked as a dental hygienist yet was able to involve herself fully with her children's interests and activities. A neighbor who had known the Connolly family for seven years described them this way: "They always did things together. Camping, sports, barbecues . . . Cindy helped prepare food for [her son's] football team. My sons went camping with them a few times."[9]

Phillip Connolly described his wife as "the perfect mother"—an opinion that was shared by many others who knew her and saw her interact with her children.[10] Cindy was widely recognized as an outgoing, exuberant woman, who was always ready to support her children and quick to prepare a sumptuous meal for friends and family.

Phillip Connolly was generally regarded as a model father and neighbor, one who deeply involved himself with his children's activities. This was particularly true for his eldest child, Daniel. On the block where the family lived, the elder Connolly had purchased and set up a basketball hoop for the neighborhood children. Friends of the Connollys' often saw Phillip and his son playing basketball together when the hoop was free. The pair also spent a good deal of time together on weekends, usually taking short hunting and fishing trips.

Daniel P. Connolly, known to all as "Danny," was considered to be an ideal teenager, who obviously loved his family and seemed to have an excellent future ahead of him. By the age of fourteen, he was a blonde, burly, nearly two-hundred-pound, baby-faced adolescent, who was admired by his peers and liked by the adults in his neighborhood. As a freshman at Esperanza High School in nearby Anaheim, Danny demonstrated an enviable talent for athletics, and despite his young age played on the school football team. Danny had also been a Little League star slugger, who had even won Most Valuable Player honors on his team. As an emerging teenager he was considered to be a fierce and relentless competitor when it came to any athletic competition, and a valued member of the teams on which he played.

Despite his wide range of interests, Danny stayed close to his family. The adolescent's friends and classmates, as well as the Connolly family neighbors, all regarded him as a stable and polite teenager who clearly demonstrated a love for both his mother and father. He was without question one of the "good kids." However, Danny also harbored a secret adolescent rage that would prove to be beyond his control and incomprehensible in its consequences.

On Thursday afternoon, February 22, 1996, Danny Connolly brutally murdered his mother in a fit of rage that was not only inexplicable but also harshly belied the teenager's

---

Snapshot Profile of Danny Connolly

A fourteen-year-old high school freshman who was raised in a close-knit, loving family. Danny was widely considered to be a happy, devoted son, close to both parents. He had a wide range of friends, was active in school sports and involved in family activities with both his mother and father. Danny had no criminal record or history of violence. In a moment of uncontrolled rage, Danny chased his mother through the family home and shot her to death. He then immediately surrendered to authorities, unable to provide an adequate explanation for his crime. The teenager was tried as a juvenile and sentenced to thirty-five years to life in prison.

entire young life and the many years of love and guidance that had been provided by his family. Most incomprehensible of all was the apparent triggering event for Danny's violent explosion—a dispute over a few missing chocolate chip cookies. However, another issue had been brewing between mother and son for some time, and that emotionally charged subject was probably at the heart of Danny's murderous outburst.

A few weeks before her murder, Cindy had grounded her son for smoking a cigarette and then lying to her about it. After he was grounded, Danny became sullen and withdrawn around the Connolly home, and he apparently complained to several of his friends at school about the disciplinary measures that Cindy had imposed. Allegedly, Danny spoke in a particularly vehement way to certain schoolmates about what he perceived to be an onerous punishment for a minor offense. A few of Danny's friends later told authorities that the adolescent had made statements that he would seek retribution against both his parents for being grounded.

However, when Danny's friends and classmates were later interviewed by reporters, most expressed genuine shock at the adolescent's extreme reaction to his mother's attempts to discipline him. It was as if they accepted and understood Danny's anger at his mother's efforts to discipline him but could not conceive of the teenager they knew so well as a murderer.

One of Danny's closest friends tried to explain away his outburst by pointing out what he believed to be an overly restrictive family environment:

He couldn't do a lot of normal things, like stay out later with the rest of our friends. Even when Danny wasn't in trouble, they'd make him stay home and sit around the house, just to be with them. He was always having to answer to his parents. He didn't like it.[11]

However, this view was singular and not voiced by others who knew Danny or his family. In fact, Danny himself never publicly expressed the opinion that his home life was unreasonably restrictive. Rather, all evidence indicates that this was not the case.

For whatever reason, Danny was unable to control the rage that burned inside him on February 22, 1996. Shortly after the teenager came home from school that afternoon, the final, fatal argument began. Danny was already angry about being grounded when Cindy apparently accused him of stealing a few cookies. The two argued loudly for a few moments, then Danny angrily left his mother in the family kitchen. He picked up a .22-caliber handgun, normally used for target shooting, and returned to the kitchen, where his mother was working at the sink, her back turned to him. Danny shot her. Severely wounded and terrified, Cindy Connolly tried to flee; however, Danny began to stalk his mother throughout the family home, firing his weapon repeatedly at her. Before the mayhem had ended, Danny had shot his mother four times. Cindy Connolly finally fell to the floor outside her master bedroom, mortally wounded. At the time of the shooting, Danny and his mother were alone in the family home. Phillip Connolly was running an errand, and Danny's younger sister, Caitlen, was at a friend's house.

Moments after shooting his mother, Danny made an emergency call to police, at 3:42. A neighbor saw the adolescent outside the Connolly home, "sobbing loudly and uncontrollably," talking on a portable telephone.[12] However, for Cindy Connolly, all help would arrive too late. She died almost immediately from her wounds.

A few moments after the emergency telephone call was received, medical and law enforcement personnel arrived at the Connolly home, to find Danny waiting for them outside. He was quickly searched for a weapon, and police began their preliminary investigation. Danny immediately confessed to shooting his mother and, sobbing, led investigating officers to the handgun that he had used to commit the crime. The teenager had thrown the weapon into an open field next to the

Connolly home. Later that afternoon Danny was arrested on suspicion of murder and held at the Orange County Juvenile Hall. Shortly after police arrived on the scene, Danny's father and Caitlen also arrived, to find patrol cars surrounding the family home, Cindy dead, and Danny in police custody.

As police investigated the crime scene they discovered a number of weapons, ranging from handguns to rifles, all legally owned but easily available to any member of the household. The teenager's father, Phillip, was an avid fisherman and hunter, who, as noted, often took his son along on weekend trips; because of this, Danny was familiar and comfortable with firearms. Unfortunately, it was one of these family-owned weapons that Danny had used to murder his mother.

During his preliminary interviews with law enforcement officials, Danny openly admitted to shooting his mother in the back with a .22-caliber handgun. However, he was not able to provide any reasonable explanation for his incredible outburst of violence. Struggling to express some relevant motive for his own actions, Danny later told the Connolly family pastor, "I couldn't take the nagging anymore."[13] Apparently, the lethal rage that exploded from the adolescent was linked to his mother's attempts to discipline him—or so Danny claimed. However, this excuse must have seemed completely beyond reason, possibly even to Danny.

In fact, it was obvious that the teenager was stunned and devastated by his own actions, and he frequently expressed this confusion and pain to others. For example, in a letter to his grandparents while being held in custody, Danny wrote: "If I could have one wish, it would be to go back in time and relive that day. I want to be back at home sitting and watching TV with Mom and Dad and Caity."[14]

No one who knew Danny could provide a reasonable explanation for his outburst, including members of his own family. His father, Phillip, confirmed to reporters that he was at a complete loss to understand what had happened to his son:

"It's like he [Danny] woke up possessed one morning and became a different kid for a day. Then he snapped out of it and it had been done, and he can't undo it."[15]

On Monday, February 26, murder charges were formally filed against Danny Connolly. The deputy district attorney, David Brent, stated that his office intended to seek permission to try the adolescent as an adult rather than in juvenile court. The prosecutor's decision was a momentous one, because Danny's case would be among the first to be tried under a new law in California that reduced the age at which adolescents could be tried as adults from sixteen to fourteen. This legal decision meant that if Danny was convicted of murder, he could face from twenty-five years to life in an adult prison, without any practical possibility of rehabilitation.

The prosecutors in Danny's case believed that the teenager had planned the murder of his mother for some time before he carried it out. According to one of the deputy district attorneys assigned to the case, Dan McNerney, Danny had told investigators that he had considered murdering his parents at least two months prior to the day of the shooting. On the day he killed his mother, Danny said he had made a twenty-dollar bet with a classmate that he would carry out his plan to murder one or both parents.

McNerney also told reporters for the *Los Angeles Times*, "During a sixth-period class, Connolly told a friend that tonight's the night," clearly implying a good deal of premeditation on the teenager's part.[16] The prosecutor went on to disclose to the media new information about the case, that Danny had retrieved and loaded a shotgun *after* murdering his mother, apparently with the intention of also killing his father when he returned home.

The implications of such apparent premeditation were stark, and if proven, would result in a virtual assurance that the adolescent's case would not be heard in juvenile court. One of the investigators in the case, Detective Terry Fincher, told reporters that many of Danny's friends had been talking about the teenager's plans to murder his mother, or both parents, and then commit suicide. Law enforcement authorities also stated that Danny had fashioned a homemade silencer out of a plastic bottle and put the device on the .22-caliber handgun that he used to shoot his mother.[17]

However, it was also obvious that on the day of the murder Danny made no effort to conceal his actions or avoid apprehension by police. In addition, his father recalled that he and his son had discussed the idea of a homemade silencer previous to Mrs. Connolly's murder and had agreed that such a device was basically useless. Even if in fact Danny had made plans to murder his mother, his entire behavior after the crime indicated an apparent absence of premeditation and a profound sense of remorse.

Perhaps the individual who knew the killer best, Danny's father, was entirely convinced that the murder of his wife was not premeditated. In an effort to spare his son from the grim scenario outlined by prosecutors in the case, Phillip Connolly immediately began making plans to lobby all who would listen to ensure that his son would not be tried as an adult.

The day after the murder of his mother, Danny Connolly first appeared in Juvenile Court and was ordered to remain in custody on the outstanding charges against him. During his brief court appearance the adolescent looked distraught and teary-eyed, unable to make eye contact with his father, who was also in attendance. Danny made no statements at the hearing.

On March 2, 1996, Phillip Connolly formally asked prosecutors not to try his son as an adult, arguing that Danny's crime was certainly not premeditated. In moving comments made to the press and public after a Sunday church service, the grieving husband and father showed a remarkable sense of forgiveness and compassion for the individual who had murdered the woman he loved: "He [Danny] needs to be responsible—as a child. What they [prosecutors] are really going to do is take away the one thing I have, and that is hope. I want him to get help. I want him to be in an environment where he can be held and nurtured."[18] Connolly also told reporters, "Part of me hates him for what he did. But he's only a boy and he needs help. We're not going to abandon him."[19] It was obvious to all who knew Danny's father that he was not only struggling with a tragedy the likes of which few could comprehend, but he was doing so with a remarkable sense of courage and understanding for his son.

Because of the intense and detailed media coverage of the crime, it became widely known that Danny Connolly was anything but a violent, aggressive juvenile. Sergeant Tom Flenniken, one of the primary investigators in the murder of Cindy Connolly, confirmed that Danny's background gave no hint of what was to come. The adolescent had no record of criminal or aggressive behavior whatsoever. For all who knew the teenager, the initial and sustained reaction to Danny's crime was one of complete shock and disbelief. However, unlike so many others, Sergeant Flenniken in his comments to the local press seemed to express a sense of resignation about the horror of what had occurred, despite Danny's unlikely background:

The kid does not have a record. He does not appear to be a problem child. [But] in my 27 years of law enforcement, nothing surprises me. Sometimes people lose it. His mother was on him and he couldn't take it anymore. He didn't want to take it anymore.[20]

Understandably, Mark Connolly, Danny's uncle, had a decidedly different reaction to Cindy Connolly's murder. Like most who knew the Connolly family, he was stunned by what had occurred: "Everybody's devastated. Total shock. He's [Danny] got no record. He's got no history of any kind of problems at all. The family—everyone's perplexed. This is the most loving family I've ever seen."[21] The sentiments expressed by Danny's uncle were echoed by virtually all who knew Danny Connolly and his family.

On June 27, 1996, Phillip Connolly received the best possible news about his son's fate: his tireless work on behalf of

Danny had been rewarded. Judge Frank F. Fasel of the Superior Court had ruled that Danny would not be tried as an adult, because he had no previous criminal record, expressed deep remorse for his actions, and was a likely candidate for rehabilitation in a youth facility. Fasel explained his actions this way: "This is not about sympathy. This is not about compassion. This hearing is about the law."[22] It was the decision that Phillip Connolly and the other family members had hoped for. However, the family now had nervously to await a decision on punishment for Danny.

In July, Judge Fasel sentenced Danny Connolly to serve thirty-five years to life in prison, to commence in a state juvenile facility. The stiff sentence was imposed in part because the adolescent had used a firearm in the commission of the crime. However, the harsh sentence gives reason for hope to Phillip Connolly and his family. Since Danny was sentenced to the California Youth Authority, it is likely that he will be released when he reaches the age of twenty-five, unless prison authorities determine that he is a continuing threat to society.

As had been his posture throughout the horrific ordeal, Phillip Connolly expressed a courageous and balanced reaction to his son's sentencing: "I'm thankful that Danny got a second chance. This is his second chance. The possibilities are up to him now."[23] However, Danny's attorney spoke to reporters of the continuing and possibly life-long impact of the adolescent's incredible moment of rage and retribution: "The legal trauma is over. Now comes the familial healing of the tragedy."[24]

Don't Tell Me What to Do

A year before Danny Connolly murdered his mother, a strikingly similar crime occurred in a setting very much like Yorba Linda, California. However, in this earlier crime, the results of teenage rage were even more gruesome.

Sharpsburg is located in Coweta County, Georgia, about thirty-five miles southwest of Atlanta. Like Yorba Linda, Sharpsburg is a settled, comfortable community with a long tradition of relatively insignificant crime and strong family values. Sadly, like its sister community to the west, this town also experienced a horrifying case of parricide, when in March 1995 Jason Lewis murdered both his parents with a shotgun.

Jason Lewis and Danny Connolly shared very similar backgrounds. Jason, who was fifteen years old when he committed murder, was widely considered to be a stable, happy adolescent, close to both parents. He had never been in trouble with the law and had no history of violence. Jason was a freshman at East Coweta High School, and to all outward appearances he had a bright and promising future. However, like most teenagers, he was not fond of the restrictions that had been placed on him by his parents, James (thirty-eight) and Ann Lewis (thirty-five).

On March 5, 1995, Jason Lewis murdered his mother and father with blasts from a shotgun while they watched television in their mobile home. Allegedly, Jason committed this heinous crime because he was angry about what he perceived to be an early curfew (midnight) that had been recently im-

---

Snapshot Profile of Jason Lewis

A fifteen-year-old high school freshman, considered stable, happy, and close to his parents. Before murdering both of them, he had no criminal record or history of violence. In a rage, Lewis murdered both parents with a shotgun while they watched television in the family home. Jason's only explanation for his crime was that he was tired of being told what to do by his mother and father. The teenager pleaded guilty to two counts of murder and was sentenced to two life terms in prison plus ten years.

posed on him by James and Ann Lewis. After shooting his parents, Jason stole $250 from his father's money clip and $40 from his mother's purse. He then fled the family trailer, carefully locked the door behind him, and made his way to a nearby friend's house.

Responding to neighbors' reports of gunfire in the area, police rushed to the scene of the double murder and soon located Jason hiding in a closet at his friend's house. Pursuing the investigation, they also discovered the shotgun Jason had used and then abandoned in the family car, parked nearby. Within moments of their arrival at the scene of his arrest, Jason Lewis confessed to police officers that he had killed his parents in a moment of uncontrollable rage.

The adolescent was taken into custody and subsequently charged with two counts of homicide, two counts of armed robbery, and a single count of possession of a firearm during the commission of a felony. Local prosecutors left no question that they intended to have the adolescent face trial as an adult, which was scheduled for November 6, 1995.

When interviewed by law enforcement officials while awaiting his trial, Jason could give no reasonable explanation for his murderous outburst. His only excuse for murder was that "he was tired of having people tell him what to do."[25] Investigators were puzzled by the Lewis murders and worked diligently to discover some logical motive for Jason's incredible actions, but they could find none. Throughout the investigation the Lewis family proved to be a fairly typical household, with no evidence of child abuse or neglect. Lieutenant Mike Kinsey, the chief investigator in the case, was baffled when it came to the question of motive: "In the case of Jason Lewis, we never came up with a real motive. What he did was so uncalled for."[26]

At least one investigator speculated that drug abuse may have played some role in Jason's crimes, although he was not under the influence of any illicit substance at the time of the murders. Jason admitted to experimenting with LSD and methamphetamine shortly before the murders. He also told a psychiatrist that he began smoking marijuana with his father when he was eight years old. However, despite the possibility of drug use, no evidence was produced that indicated Jason Lewis was addicted to illicit substances or alcohol. It is more likely that the teenager was suffering from significant depression and a strong sense of isolation at the time he murdered his parents—conditions that were formally diagnosed by the psychiatrist with whom Jason had the conversation about drug use.

Before Jason Lewis appeared for trial, he pleaded guilty to all charges against him. In early November 1995 he was sentenced to two consecutive life terms plus ten years in prison. During the hearing to determine his sentence, the teenager was allowed to make a statement to the presiding judge; he said, "I would just like to say to my family and friends that I'm sorry. I'm not going to make any excuses for this, but I want to say I love you and I'm sorry."[27] Throughout the proceedings, Jason's demeanor ranged from impassive to tearful during testimony given on his behalf by his sister.

Like Danny Connolly, Jason Lewis had no reason to murder and could not find within himself a reasonable explanation for his crimes. In both cases, the murdering adolescent became uncontrollably enraged and lashed out against his loved ones in an act of unspeakable violence. Neither Connolly nor Lewis were prone to violence or uncontrolled aggressive behavior. However, despite their ordinary, stable backgrounds, both committed monstrous acts against those closest to them, each because of a hidden, overwhelming rage, and each in an unrestrained, uncontrolled search for the ultimate form of retribution.

BEYOND RAGE TO PREMEDITATION

The cases of Danny Connolly and Jason Lewis are not necessarily typical of the crime of parricide, although they are representative of the chaos, confusion, and pain that almost always surrounds this frightening felony. In such cases there is always the important and omnipresent question of premeditation to be considered. From a prosecutor's point of view, the possibility of premeditation is an essential issue, if the crime is to be considered a capital offense and the juvenile is to be tried as an adult. Therefore, when crimes of parricide are investigated prosecutors actively seek out any evidence of premeditation in an effort to determine the state of mind of the murderer when the crime was committed.

Often, as in the case of Danny Connolly, an adolescent perpetrator has made statements to peers that seem to indicate premeditation in the murder of one or both parents. This was clearly the situation in the Connolly case, who had spoken openly to friends about the deep anger he was experiencing toward his parents. Premeditation may have also played a part in the Lewis case. Subsequent to Jason Lewis's arrest, officials arrested three of the perpetrator's friends on suspicion that they had plotted the crime with him. All three were later tried in juvenile court, but only one was convicted (of obstruction)—the adolescent who had agreed to hide Jason Lewis in his closet after the murders. As in most cases of parricide, evidence of premeditation is an elusive prey, which even when discovered can be interpreted in many different ways.

It is not unusual for adolescents who murder one or more of their parents to have complained of dissatisfaction prior to committing the crime. These teenagers often share their grievances with their friends or classmates on a routine basis. However, many more teenagers complain about the unreasonableness of their parents than resort to killing them. The fact that an adolescent complains bitterly about his parents, or even threatens in the presence of friends to kill them, does not necessarily indicate that he or she will do so. Still, the fact remains that such spoken statements, even if they are clearly only braggadocio, can form the basis for a legal presumption of premeditation to a subsequent crime.

In most instances of parricide committed by a teenager, the final arbiter of punishment is a judge. Most of these cases are not heard by a jury, and most defendants are not tried as adults. The question of premeditation is therefore often the object of subjective determination by a single individual—the judge who hears the case. Clearly, this is a delicate and difficult responsibility for any individual to assume. In the final analysis, a judge must determine if the angry statements made before the crime were indicative of premeditation or were something less sinister. This is clearly not a decision that can be made easily, in most cases.

In the company of friends or classmates, many adolescents threaten to harm their parents when the subject of parental guidance arises. Obviously, not many teenagers physically harm or murder their parents. How are we to know when such threatening statements evidence premeditation and when they are simply expressions of anger and frustration without violent intent? Just as we have yet to come to an understanding of why adolescent rage can lead to the ultimate form of violence, we have yet to know our children well enough to consistently and accurately judge the essential meaning of their angry statements. However, of this we can be sure: adolescent statements of any intent to harm or murder any other individual, especially parents, must be taken very seriously. Even though such statements may be nothing more than schoolyard bravado designed purely to impress a teenager's peer group, who among us would want to make such a foolhardy assumption?

A CONTRACT FOR MURDER

Although most crimes of parricide are committed by a raging adolescent in the privacy of the family home and without a clear motive, there are exceptions to this troubling profile. In a few instances, the murder of parents is clearly premeditated and motivated by something far more concrete than adolescent rage. One example is the 1992 case of Kristi Anne

Koslow, who not only gave a great deal of thought to the murder of her father and stepmother but meticulously arranged a contract for their execution—and all for profit. However, despite her heinous crime, Kristi had never been considered a violent teenager, hell-bent on murder. Her actions were as unexpected and shocking as those of Danny Connolly or Jason Lewis.

Kristi was born on Valentine's Day in 1975, and was adopted a few days after her birth by Jack and Paula Koslow, of Fort Worth, Texas. At the time of Kristi's adoption the Koslows had been married for five years, but they had been unable to have children of their own. When Kristi was six years old the Koslow marriage collapsed, and the couple filed for divorce. Kristi was placed in her adoptive mother's custody, and Jack was given visitation rights. Two years after his divorce Jack Koslow married Caren Courtney, who worked with him at a local bank. They lived in an affluent area of the city, and soon after the marriage Caren quit her job and became prominent in Fort Worth social circles. During this time, Kristi and her adoptive mother lived only a few blocks from Koslow, a businessman, and his second wife, but Kristi was only an occasional visitor. Over the next few years, Paula and Jack would sometimes be at opposite ends of arguments about Kristi's welfare and support. Unfortunately, Kristi was well aware of the tension between her adoptive mother and father, and she became increasingly angry toward Jack Koslow, Caren, and about their comfortable, affluent lifestyle. Kristi would often become verbally hostile in the presence of Jack's wife.

At home with Paula, Kristi developed into an angry teenager, who would sometimes vent her rage at her adoptive mother. On at least two occasions Kristi ran away from home, but she quickly returned. However, despite the anger of her adolescent years, the teenager had no criminal record and no history of violence. No one could have anticipated that Kristi Anne Koslow's secret rage and compulsion for retribution would run so deep that she would plot the death of Jack and Caren Koslow and see the plan through to its conclusion.

On the morning of March 12, 1992, before dawn, Jack Koslow frantically pounded on a neighbor's door, pleading for help. He had been viciously beaten, stabbed in the neck with a large knife, and was bleeding profusely. Fortunately, Koslow would survive his wounds; however, as he was receiving emergency medical attention, Koslow's wife already lay dead in the family home.

When police responded to Jack Koslow's emergency call, he was able to tell them only that two unidentified men had broken into the family home and attacked the couple in their bedroom. Caren Koslow had been brutally beaten, and her throat had been slit. On the floor near his wife's body, police discovered a knife from the kitchen that had been used in the attack.

In the early stages of the investigation, police were baffled by the crime. Nothing was missing from the Koslow home except Jack's wallet; robbery was soon ruled out as a motive.

Snapshot Profile of Kristi Anne Koslow

The sixteen-year-old daughter of divorced parents, who stayed in contact with both her adoptive father and mother. Although she had no criminal record or history of violence, Kristi had become increasingly angry over the separation of her parents and envious of the affluent lifestyle of her adoptive father and stepmother. Koslow planned their murder and convinced two other teenagers (one of them her boyfriend) to carry out the plan. During the attack, Koslow's stepmother was murdered, but her father survived. In the course of the investigation, the two teenagers who attacked the Koslows surrendered to police and confessed that Koslow had planned the murder so that she would inherit her father's estate. Koslow was brought to trial and found guilty of murder.

Jack Koslow was unable to provide a detailed description of his attackers. However, he did recall being startled from sleep by the noise of someone kicking in his bedroom door. Koslow had instinctively leapt from his bed and had run to a closet in the adjoining dressing room to retrieve his shotgun. However, before he was able to reach it the attackers ordered him back into the bedroom, where they forced the couple to lay face down on the floor. The unidentified intruders then proceeded to beat Koslow into unconsciousness, stab him in the neck, and murder his wife.

As the investigation proceeded, Jack Koslow became a suspect in the murder of his wife, largely on the basis of forensic evidence—bite marks on his hands—that could have been inflicted by Caren during a struggle. The medical examiner also questioned the time of Caren's death, suggesting that it could have happened hours earlier than reported by her husband. The implication was that Jack Koslow could have murdered his wife earlier that night and then covered the crime by inflicting wounds upon himself. Although the scenario seemed an unlikely one on the surface, police took the opinions of the medical examiner seriously and began investigating Koslow as a primary suspect. Despite these accusations, Koslow cooperated completely with authorities and did not hire an attorney in his own defense. Fortunately, he was proved to be uninvolved in the murder of his wife when police received a tip that would radically change the course of their investigation and stun those who knew the Koslow family.

Two weeks after Caren Koslow's murder, friends of Kristi's confessed to the horrible attack. A police informant provided information to authorities that two local teenagers had asked him to dispose of a wallet and credit cards belonging to Jack Koslow. The individuals who wanted to fence Koslow's property were close friends of his daughter, Kristi. When police followed up on the tip, the two adolescents quickly confessed to their role in the attack on Jack and Caren. The teenagers stated that Kristi Anne Koslow had contracted with them for the murder of Jack and Caren Koslow; she had agreed to pay them $500,000 once they had completed their gruesome work. After the agreement for murder had been concluded, Kristi had prepared a detailed floor plan of the Koslow residence and had given them the security code to the home alarm system.

The two teenage murderers were Jeffrey Dillingham and Brian Salter, Kristi's boyfriend. According to statements made by Dillingham and Salter, Kristi had dominated the relationship with Salter and had been easily able to bend him to her will, including convincing him to commit murder. On the basis of their uneven, deadly relationship, Kristi had been able to persuade Salter to help her arrange for the murder of her father and stepmother with Dillingham's assistance. Salter had cooperated because he believed he would receive a portion of the estate of Jack Koslow when he eventually married Kristi. Dillingham was to be paid in cash for his role in the crime.

The three adolescents had made meticulous plans to carry out the murders, with Kristi Anne Koslow arranging the details as necessary. According to prosecutors in the case against Kristi and the other adolescents, the motive for murder was straightforward and indisputable—greed. However, for Kristi, there were two additional reasons for murder: rage and retribution.

In August 1993 Jeffrey Dillingham was tried, found guilty of first-degree murder, and sentenced to death. One month later, Brian Salter pleaded guilty to the same charge and was given a life sentence. Salter had agreed to testify against Kristi Anne Koslow at her trial, in exchange for his life. In June 1994, a Fort Worth jury found Kristi guilty of murder, after a little more than three hours' deliberation. Jack Koslow was in attendance during the closing arguments at Kristi's trial and when the jury returned their verdict. After the court proceedings, the father of the defendant expressed to reporters his belief that the verdict of the jury was fair and appropriate. Kristi was subsequently sentenced to life in prison.

Mark Daniel, Koslow's attorney, had fought vigorously

against the ultimate verdict and felt that Kristi should not have been found guilty of murder. He remained convinced that his client should only have been found guilty of a lesser crime: "It's frightening when the state seeks the death penalty for a defendant with no prior criminal history, who is 17 years of age, [and] who by any person's account did not actually cause the death of anybody."

Clearly the jury did not agree with the defendant's position. From its point of view, Kristi was as culpable as Dillingham and Salter in the murder of Caren Koslow and the attack on her husband. There can be little doubt that the defendant's actions in plotting against her family and arranging the details of their execution were viewed by the jury as clear evidence of premeditated murder.

The case of Kristi Anne Koslow is extremely unusual in that children rarely murder their parents for money or possessions. In the Koslow case, it seems evident that the perpetrator's actions were also motivated by an overwhelming sense of anger, alienation, and envy of her father's success. These emotions were clearly some of the driving forces behind Kristi Koslow's murderous plot. However, this crime proved exceptional in other ways as well. It is also unusual for an adolescent contemplating the murder of his or her parents to actively involve another teenager in the commission of the crime, even though the perpetrator often discusses the plan with friends or classmates. However, as is obvious from the murder of Caren Koslow and the attack on her husband, cases of premeditated murder by an otherwise nonviolent adolescent can occur, even with such a disturbing and unusual motive as greed playing a crucial role, and even with peers recruited to carry out the gruesome deed.

FRIENDS AND LOVERS

Adolescence is a time of enormous change, learning, pain, pleasure, and upheaval, even under the best of circumstances.

As a child enters his or her teenage years, a realignment of relationships becomes inevitable—and apparent. There also arises a perceptible and sometimes troubling struggle to identify and assert the adolescent's unique personality and role in his or her family, with his or her peers, and in society. Throughout these turbulent years emotions often run high, life experiences are frequently profound, and the ways of living and loving undergo significant and rapid transformations. It is in the teenage years that individuals reassess the role of their parents and develop important new personal relationships with members of their peer group. In many cases these friendships last a lifetime, because they develop at such a critical point in an adolescent's life. It is also during this time that the teenager first experiences the overwhelming impact of sexual love—something very different from anything he or she ever experienced as a child.

It is common for a teenager to declare a particular peer as a "best friend." In some cases the adolescent publicly recognizes several individuals as best friends. However, he or she is likely to be especially close to a single friend, usually of the same sex and approximately the same age, with whom the most personal secrets can be shared and in whom he or she places absolute trust. These intimate relationships not only are vital to adolescent development, but they can be sources of intense disappointment and pain when they are marred by disputes, jealousy, or dishonesty.

If a teenager places his or her absolute trust in a special friend who then commits some offense that threatens to destroy the relationship, there naturally arises a profound sense of hurt, which seems to be especially difficult for adolescents. In part, this anguish may come about because of the resulting deep feeling of abandonment at a time when many, if not all, the teenager's relationships are undergoing scrutiny and change. In any case, when a special relationship collapses the adolescent's disappointment, pain, and anger can be intense.

From a parent's point of view, it may seem relatively

simple and obvious to counsel their son or daughter to try to resolve the dispute that caused a breach in an important friendship. Parents may advise their child to move on to another relationship, pointing out that all human interaction is fraught with the possibility of misunderstanding and change. However, from a teenager's point of view matters are not so simple, and resolutions are not so easily seen. The destruction of an important relationship can be completely devastating and life changing. Even the most caring, well-intentioned parental advice about such a disaster can seem superficial and insensitive to the pained and confused teenager. Fortunately, with the caring support of family, most adolescents are able to move beyond the pain of losing a best friend and soon adapt to the constantly changing, intricate relationships that are fundamental components of growing up.

However, in a few cases, the collapse of an intimate friendship can evoke the kind of uncontrollable rage and need for retribution that sometimes results in murder. When such a dangerous situation arises, "retribution" can be swift and lethal, even at the hands of a teenager who would not otherwise consider violence and who valued his or her special relationship with the victim beyond all others. The case of Jeremy Hernandez typifies the horrible disasters that can result from the collapse of an intimate friendship.

The Price of Spreading Rumors

Jeremy Hernandez and Samuel Dean Atkins were obviously best friends. Hernandez, seventeen years old, and Atkins, sixteen years old, attended Paso Robles High School, in Paso Robles, California, together and enjoyed most of the same activities and adventures. One of the duo's favorite pastimes was to roam the Cypress Mountain Road area north of where they lived with their rifles, in search of wild turkey. During these excursions they would also drink a few beers and share the intimate camaraderie of best friends.

However, in the spring of 1996, the close relationship between Hernandez and Atkins began to deteriorate. Hernandez learned that his best friend had apparently been spreading rumors at their high school that Hernandez was gay. To Jeremy, this was the worst form of insult, and it was coming from a person whom he had trusted completely. Hernandez was devastated at Sam's apparent act of treachery. He felt hurt, betrayed, and furious, and he was unwilling to overlook the rumors. However, when he directly approached Atkins about the insults, the younger teenager denied any involvement. Jeremy was not convinced, and he certainly was not willing to forgive and forget.

On May 16, 1996, Hernandez invited Atkins to join him on a turkey-shooting, beer-drinking adventure. Prior to the trip, Jeremy purchased ammunition for his shotgun at a local Wal-Mart; in fact, he purchased the most powerful ammunition that the store carried. Atkins brought a single-shot rifle, and the teenagers headed in Jeremy's car for the remote area known locally as Cypress Mountain, or Klau Mine Road.

Sometime after Hernandez and Atkins arrived at their destination, the two argued about the rumors that had been spread at school, both armed with their respective rifles. In what a psychiatrist later described as "an emotional explosion," Jeremy suddenly attacked his friend, disarmed him, and emptied his shotgun into Atkins's body—a total of five powerful

---

Snapshot Profile of Jeremy Hernandez

A seventeen-year-old high school student without any criminal record or history of violence. In a moment of uncontrollable rage, Hernandez brutally murdered his sixteen-year-old best friend because he heard that his friend had been spreading rumors about him at school. After the murder, Hernandez surrendered to authorities. He was brought to trial as a juvenile and found guilty of first-degree murder.

blasts.[28] He then retrieved Atkins's single-shot, .22-caliber rifle and shot his severely wounded friend in the face. Incredibly, Hernandez then reloaded the rifle and shot Atkins yet again, this time in the side of his forehead. Atkins died at the scene, of seven gunshot wounds.

As soon as the gruesome attack ended, Hernandez jumped in his car and fled the scene, driving over Samuel Atkins's body in the process. Sometime later he wiped the weapons clean of fingerprints, discarded them, and checked into a nearby motel under an assumed name. However, Jeremy was devastated and frightened by what he had done, and he desperately needed to talk to someone he trusted. The day after the shooting Hernandez confessed the crime to his grandfather, who easily convinced the teenager to surrender voluntarily to authorities. On the day Jeremy Hernandez surrendered and was preliminarily charged with murder, he was just a month shy of his eighteenth birthday.

Like so many teenagers whose uncontrollable rage drives them to murder, Hernandez had no prior criminal history and had not been considered a violent individual. However, because he was nearly eighteen at the time of the crime and had committed such a brutal, senseless killing, prosecutors demanded that the adolescent face trial as an adult. Whether or not Hernandez would be directed to the juvenile court system was crucial to his future. If tried as an adult and found guilty, he could be sentenced to thirty years to life in prison, without any possibility of rehabilitation; however, if tried in juvenile court, the teenager would be held only until he was twenty-five years old, and he would receive counseling during his imprisonment. This crucial decision rested with the judge in the case, who was charged with determining whether or not the teenager was a promising candidate for rehabilitation and unlikely to pose a threat to society in the future.

Probation officers and psychiatrists interviewed Jeremy Hernandez extensively, as did police investigators and prosecutors, to formulate their respective recommendations to the judge. In August 1996 a hearing was held before Judge Michael Duffy of Juvenile Court to determine Hernandez's fate at trial. The probation officer assigned to Jeremy recommended to the judge that the case remain in the juvenile court system. Describing Hernandez's reaction to the rumors allegedly spread by his best friend, the probation officer said, "He [Hernandez] was devastated by this, that his best friend would call him names at school. From his perspective, [it was] the worst thing that he could be called."[29] The probation officer argued that Hernandez should receive intensive counseling, that he was an ideal candidate for rehabilitation, and he was unlikely to act violently in the future. He also presented strong evidence, some of it from psychiatrists, that indicated the teenager had lashed out in a moment of uncontrollable rage and that after the crime had demonstrated profound remorse for his actions.

Prosecutors attempted to paint a much darker portrait of the perpetrator. According to their arguments, Jeremy had carefully planned the murder of his friend and had made obvious efforts to conceal the crime. In essence, the prosecution described Hernandez as a cold-blooded, calculating killer who had deliberately lured his friend into the remote area in order to complete a well-planned crime of homicide.

For his part, Jeremy Hernandez gave conflicting versions of what had occurred on May 16, 1996. However, he did express significant remorse about his actions. He also told his probation officer that he had had no idea he was going to shoot Atkins until the moment he first pulled the trigger of the shotgun. After that, according to his interpretation of what occurred, he was out of control and unable to stop shooting. Many who interviewed the teenager agreed with this view.

After hearing both arguments, Judge Duffy decided that Jeremy Hernandez, although he was now eighteen, should be kept in the juvenile court system and not be tried as an adult. Duffy's decision was based on the absence of any criminal history and the testimony strongly indicating that Hernandez had been in an uncontrollable rage at the time of the murder. Duffy's decision clearly refuted the prosecution's position that the teenager had willfully planned and carried out the murder of his best friend.

In October 1996, Jeremy Hernandez was found guilty of first-degree murder in a juvenile court and was remanded to the California Youth Authority. He will be held there for up to seven years, when he will probably be freed, at the age of twenty-five. To those who knew Jeremy Hernandez and those who testified on his behalf, it is clear that the young man committed a crime so forcign to his nature and so unexpected that only overwhelming rage could account for his actions. However, for the family and friends of Samuel Atkins, such an explanation can provide little or no solace for their horrendous loss.

Jeremy and Brad

On November 10, 1995, Rhonda Michie, the frightened mother of thirteen-year-old Brad Hansen, telephoned police in Arizona to report her son's disappearance. Earlier that day Michie had gone to work as usual, believing that her son was preparing to go to school. However, she had later realized that it was Veteran's Day, a school holiday, and she had tried to reach Brad on his pager to learn his whereabouts. The boy had never answered the page and had not been at home when Michie returned from work. Concerned and confused, Brad's mother telephoned police to report him as a possible runaway.

On that morning in November, Brad went about his usual routine in his usual way, quietly allowing his mother to believe that Centennial Middle School was in session. However, the thirteen-year-old had already made other plans. He had arranged to spend the day with his best friend, Jeremy Bach, also thirteen years old, a classmate at the middle school. Shortly after his mother left for work Brad bicycled to his friend's house, arriving a few minutes before seven in the morning. He was greeted and let in by Jeremy's father, who was on his way to work.

Later that morning, Brad Hansen lay dying in the Bach home of a single gunshot wound. What transpired during those few, final moments of Brad's life may never be known with certainty, but there is sufficient evidence and testimony to piece together a fairly accurate synopsis of the gruesome events of that morning.

Jeremy Bach initially told investigating officers that Brad had accidentally shot himself to death during an argument between the teenagers. Convinced (as he later claimed) that his friend was already dead from the self-inflicted wound, and in a panic, Jeremy had placed Brad's body in the family's curbside trash container, which was later picked up by the local sanitation company. Sadly, Brad Hansen's body was subsequently dumped in an unknown location in a landfill. However, as the investigation into Brad's death and disappearance proceeded, this story made little sense to authorities, because Jeremy had waited for two hours after the shooting before dumping his friend's body into the trash container. Jeremy told investigators that he had spent that time thoroughly cleaning the house and disposing of cigarettes that he and Brad had been smoking.

On December 13 Jeremy told investigators that he and Brad had been at the Bach home since early on the morning of the shooting. They had watched television and listened to music for about twenty minutes. At that point, according to Jeremy, the two teenagers began to argue about a female schoolmate—a heated, angry dispute that ended with Jeremy retrieving a handgun that had been hidden under the cushions of a couch, where it was always kept by his father. Jeremy now asserted that his hand had accidentally bumped against a nearby table, discharging a single shot from the weapon. According to Jeremy's revised version of events, the bullet struck his best friend and killed him. However, by his own admission, Jeremy had not immediately called police or emergency medical services, nor had he been sure that his best friend was already dead. Rather, he then spent two hours cleaning up the crime scene, while his friend actually lay dying on the floor. Later, allegedly still in a panic, Jeremy disposed of Brad's body in the family trash container.

Throwing Jeremy's latest explanation into further doubt was the testimony of the girl who had been the subject of the argument between the two friends. Sometime after ten that morning, she had dropped by Jeremy's house to visit the two boys, apparently knowing they would be there. Jeremy told her that he and Brad had just gotten into an argument and that Brad had fired a shot at him, but missed. Jeremy explained Brad's absence by telling the girl that Brad had hurriedly left on his bicycle, leaving behind his favorite hat and his pager. According to the girl's later statements to police, Jeremy had shown her a bullet hole in the kitchen wall of the home to convince her of the truth of his story.

Investigators were understandably suspicious about Jeremy Bach's explanation of his friend's death and the inconsistencies in his story. However, at first they were hampered by the absence of the victim's body and any convincing forensic evidence. Throughout December 1995 police conducted extensive interviews and repeated searches for additional facts and evidence, but the case remained weak.

On January 9, 1996, law enforcement officers asked the

Snapshot Profile of Jeremy Bach

A thirteen-year-old who had no criminal record and no history of violence. In a heated argument with his best friend, Jeremy shot and killed the thirteen-year-old. He then disposed of the victim's body in the family trash container. During the investigation into the shooting, Jeremy gave conflicting stories to authorities and was subsequently arrested. He was charged with second-degree murder and ordered to stand trial as an adult.

Phoenix Sanitation Department to help with their investigation by switching the garbage can used by Jeremy Bach to dispose of his friend's body with another, identical container. Retrieving the suspect garbage container, forensic technicians discovered a large area of bloodstains. The blood was soon determined to belong to Brad Hansen. On February 15, based on the mounting forensic evidence, a search warrant was issued to allow police to investigate Jeremy's home. Police quickly located a .357 Magnum revolver that had been hidden in a masonry planter under some artificial plants. They believed this to be the weapon that had been used to murder Brad Hansen.

With convincing evidence now in hand, authorities charged Jeremy Bach with second-degree murder and had him extradited from Las Vegas, where he had been living with his mother since November 1995. By the first week of March Jeremy was in custody at a juvenile detention facility in Mesa, Arizona; a preliminary hearing had been scheduled for later in the month.

On March 2, a moving memorial service was held for Brad Hansen, despite the fact that his body had not yet been located. Many of the teenager's classmates from Centennial Middle School wrote emotional letters and tributes to their lost companion. Over 350 friends and acquaintances of Brad and his family attended the service. On that day Brad's mother, Rhonda Michie, and his stepfather, Jerry Michie, sorrowfully recalled a young teenager who had been filled with life, had been very popular with schoolmates, and had obviously had a bright future.

During the service Brad's family reasserted their commitment to have the teenager's remains found. However, that was not to be.

That month, the city council was asked by the mayor to authorize at least $100,000 of city funds to continue the search for Brad Hansen's body. It was hoped that if Brad's remains could be found, a forensic anthropologist could provide additional information about his death. Nonetheless, despite the absence of remains, prosecutors were convinced that they had more than sufficient evidence to proceed to trial. In any case, few officials involved in the continuing search for Brad's remains thought they would ever be found. One of the investigators in the case spoke for the others when questioned about the difficult and expensive prospective search: "We thought that the case is clearly prosecutable without a body. It is also unlikely that if such a search took place that the body would ever be found. The best we could hope for is to maybe find a bone of the body."[30] However, the unspoken issue on the minds of those involved in the investigation was to bring some closure for the grieving parents of Brad Hansen.

In May 1996, despite the failure to locate any remains, Jeremy Bach was ordered to stand trial as an adult by a Maricopa County superior judge. The decision for the judge was a difficult one, in part because the defendant had no criminal record and no prior history of violent behavior. The thirteen-year-old was held on $100,000 bond, and an arraignment date was set for later that month. At the time of his incarceration Jeremy Bach was the youngest inmate in the Maricopa County jail system. However, his bond was quickly placed, and the teenager was released to the custody of his parents to await his trial.

Prior to the judge's decision, Rhonda Michie had publicly lobbied that the killer of her son be tried as an adult. In emotional testimony before the court, Brad's mother explained her position this way: "This was no accident. Jeremy had two opportunities to save our son's life—he chose not to. If Jeremy Bach is not transferred to an adult court, he has gotten away with murder."[31] In November 1997, Bach was found guilty of second-degree murder, making history as the youngest person ever to stand trial for homicide in Arizona. Two months later, he was sentenced to twenty-two years in prison.

FROM LOVE TO RETRIBUTION

How can a lifelong, supposedly loving relationship, like that between a child and his or her parents, be suddenly transformed into a senseless act of murder? How can an otherwise nonviolent teenager kill his best friend in a moment of fury that seems utterly insane? Why do these crimes happen, and how can they occur with such abruptness and vicious results?

If we ask the perpetrators of these crimes why they killed a parent, family member, or best friend, they can rarely explain their actions in a comprehensible way. The case of Gavin Mandin provides an excruciating but common example of the inability of a young perpetrator to reasonably explain the motivations for his crime.

In 1991, at the age of fifteen, Mandin murdered his mother, stepfather, and two younger sisters in their family home in Canada. The teenager shot each family member with a .22-caliber rifle and disposed of the bodies in a brushy area behind the Mandin home. As is typical in cases of parricide, no one had expected the teenager to lash out with such incredible violence against his own family. When stunned investigators listened to Mandin's confession, he told them that he had murdered his family because he hated doing the household chores that were a routine part of his responsibilities. Beyond this fantastic explanation, the teenager showed no remorse for his crimes; he said to officers, "I guess I get the house now, eh?"[32]

Such an explanation for murder is obviously incredible and ludicrous. It is also extremely disturbing, as was the apparent lack of remorse demonstrated by Gavin Mandin. However, it is often foolhardy to take at face value the statements made by these young killers to interrogating officers. No one would doubt that Gavin Mandin hated the chores he was given by his parents. Such a reaction is normal and predictable for many teenagers. It is to be expected that an adolescent will shun what he or she perceives to be distasteful chores. For a teenager to be argumentative, noncompliant, and unenthusiastic about things he or she does not favor is not surprising and does not imply a violent reaction. However, when this normal reluctance or avoidance becomes transformed into a pathology that leads to murder, we cannot rest with an acceptance of the obvious. We must try to search out why occasionally an adolescent becomes so obsessed and controlled by his escalating rage that a household chore or a minor argument with his mother becomes the only motivation he can provide for murder.

A common explanation for this kind of crime is that the perpetrator is in essence an individual without a conscience. This argument is tantamount to saying that the teenager who commits parricide or murders his best friend is in actuality a sociopath—a person who cannot feel or express remorse or concern for the welfare of others, because he is truly incapable of experiencing such emotions. In psychiatric terms, this is a person suffering from *antisocial personality disorder*, also referred to by such terms as *psychopathy, sociopathy,* or *dissocial personality disorder*.

Although this explanation may be true in some cases of teenage parricide, it is a relatively rare circumstance and one that would not apply to the adolescents discussed in this book. According to the American Psychiatric Association (APA), "the essential feature of Antisocial Personality Disorder is a pervasive pattern of disregard for, and violation of, the rights of others that begins in childhood or early adolescence and

---

Snapshot Profile of Gavin Mandin

A fifteen-year-old Canadian who had no history of violence or criminal activities. In a rage, he murdered his father, mother, and two sisters with a rifle in their family home. When investigators asked the teenager why he had committed such a brutal, senseless crime, he answered that he was tired of doing the household chores given him by his parents.

continues into adulthood."[33] Current APA standards dictate that this disorder cannot be formally diagnosed unless the individual has reached the age of eighteen and has exhibited significant evidence of conduct disorder since at least the age of fifteen, among other criteria:[34]

- A pervasive disregard for, and violation of, the rights of others occurring since the age of fifteen years, indicated by three or more of the following:
  1. Failure to conform to social norms and repeatedly performing acts that are grounds for arrest
  2. Repeated lying and habitual deceitfulness
  3. Impulsivity
  4. Chronic irritability and aggressiveness
  5. Reckless disregard for the safety of self or others
  6. Consistent irresponsibility
  7. Lack of remorse for harmful actions
- The individual must be at least eighteen years of age.

Our contemporary understanding of this type of personality disorder is that it is usually associated with individuals from a low socioeconomic background and dense urban environments. Antisocial personality disorder is also known to be much more common in males than females; statistically, this disorder is found in about 3 percent of males and 1 percent of females in the United States.

While antisocial personality disorder may lie at the root of some instances of otherwise unexplained adolescent murder, it is clearly not a serious consideration in most cases. Much has been made in the media about kids who are hell bent on a life of violence and mayhem, such as one would expect of a sociopath. However, in reality antisocial personality disorder is simply not very prevalent among adolescents. Many teenagers commit murder unexpectedly and without any history of such a long-term psychiatric disorder.

Another line of explanation points to cases of parricide in which the offender was a horribly abused, neglected, or abandoned child. There is no question that a childhood filled with this kind of dysfunction and pain can lead to murder. In fact, there are many such instances in the literature. However, there are also many cases in which there was no overt evidence of childhood abuse, neglect, or abandonment. Those who strongly subscribe to an abusive childhood as a prerequisite for parricide often argue that children subjected to horrible experiences go on to murder a parent without this mitigating information ever being disclosed. There is no doubt that in some cases this is true. Childhood abuse and neglect is a horrifying and closely held secret in our society, and its victims often suffer all their lives without publicly disclosing the true terror of their childhood. However, it is also true that most households are not abusive. The literature of the crime of parricide clearly indicates that many perpetrators grew up in stable, loving, very ordinary families, where abuse, abandonment, and neglect never occurred.

It is also argued that children who murder a parent, family member, or close friend often witnessed violence within the family throughout their childhood. According to this theory, the teenager comes to accept violence as routine, even though abhorrent. Under such conditions, it is said, an adolescent may be more prone to react with physical violence against others, including his or her parents, and such violence can quickly escalate to murder. Once again, this is a solid and believable argument. There *are* cases of parricide in which the background of the perpetrator substantiates the essential role of previous family violence in the crime. However, as with each of the other persuasive theories about this crime, there are as many exceptions as there are incidents to substantiate it.

Finally, we must fully recognize the extraordinary impact of alcohol and drugs on our sons and daughters. Although the number of adolescents who regularly use alcohol or drugs has decreased in the last decade, this is still a pervasive problem across the United States. In fact, our society is awash in alcohol and drugs, in both urban and suburban areas of the country. We are also awash in conflicting studies about this problem and its impact on our children. However, all reasonable studies agree that the use of alcohol and drugs by adolescents can lead to more aggressive behavior and higher rates of crime, regardless of the socioeconomic status of the individuals who use these substances.

Despite the alarming number of adolescents who use alcohol and drugs, however, not all teenage murderers are under the influence of these substances when they commit their crimes. A review of the case histories in this book makes it clear that many murders by adolescents are committed without any hint of the use of alcohol or drugs. As is said of antisocial personality disorder, it is a common perception that adolescents who kill *must* be addicted to alcohol, drugs, or both. However, it is often the case that these perpetrators are not victims of such an addiction, and in many cases are not even users of these substances.

From time to time we learn of an act of murder committed by an adolescent who seemed to be suffering from a long-term psychological disorder that may have played a significant role in his or her crime. Often, these alleged mental illnesses are controversial, and in some cases vague in their meaning to a judge or jury. Unless such a disorder is profound and obvious, the American legal system is slow to accept such an illness as a mitigating circumstance in a crime as egregious as homicide.

In cases where rage and retribution are clear, even if there is also evidence of mental aberration, prosecutors are compelled to seek the harshest punishment possible in view of the frequently horrific nature of the crime and the inevitable public outcry. Such was the case with a California teenager, Joshua Jenkins, in 1996.

At the age of fifteen, in February 1996, Jenkins murdered five members of his family, in an incredible display of brutality and viciousness. The teenager used a hammer, a kitchen knife, and an ax to kill his grandparents, parents, and his ten-year-old sister. Jenkins dragged their bodies into the master bedroom of their condominium and set the residence on fire. He then escaped from the crime scene in the family car. However, the adolescent was quickly arrested and charged with five counts of first-degree homicide.

When interrogators tried to determine a motive for the brutal killings, Jenkins was unable to provide any rational explanation, other than to express repeatedly a sustained rage at his parents. His fuming anger had apparently taken on new dimensions after he was placed in a private boarding school because of his history of unpredictable and sometimes aggressive behavior. In later conversations with investigators and medical personnel, Jenkins also often referred to anger and confusion about being an adopted child as a possible motivating issue. However, in the final analysis, the teenager never pointed to a specific reason for killing his family, especially, his younger sister, whom he claimed to love deeply.

Prosecutors were adamant that Jenkins should be tried as an adult because of the especially heinous nature of the murders. The district attorney prosecuting the case said this about the teenager's crime and his desire to try Jenkins as an adult: "This is a level of gruesomeness that is virtually indescribable.

Snapshot Profile of Joshua Jenkins

A fifteen-year-old who had a long history of bizarre, unpredictable, and sometimes aggressive behavior. After being placed in a special boarding school because of his psychological problems, Jenkins murdered five members of his family in an incredible display of brutality. Despite the fact he was later diagnosed as mentally ill by several psychologists and psychiatrists, Jenkins was eventually found to be sane at the time of the murders and sentenced to 112 years in prison.

I see no argument why someone who commits such serial murders should not be tried as an adult."[35] Because of his age and the existing laws in California at that time, the decision to try the teenager as an adult could not result in the death penalty. However, Jenkins could face a sentence of from twenty-five years to life for each of the five counts of murder against him.

Joshua Jenkins was a large and burly teenager, who had a history of behavioral problems that extended into his childhood. Prior to the murders, as noted, he had been placed in a private school in southern California because he had exhibited bizarre, unruly, and sometimes violent outbursts. He was also known to be subject to wild swings of mood, which often ranged from friendly to aggressive in a matter of moments. Prior to his attendance at the Vista Del Mar school in California, Jenkins had been enrolled in a series of special education classes in a Las Vegas school, where his grandparents lived. However, he had been a constant source of disruption in class, and his stay at the school ended abruptly in a violent fight with another student.

A year after his arrest, in April 1997, Jenkins pleaded guilty to five counts of murder, setting aside an earlier plea of not guilty by reason of insanity. Prior to his final plea the teenager had been extensively examined by a number of psychologists and psychiatrists, who agreed that he was mentally ill. However, no consensus was reached about whether Jenkins was legally sane or insane. With a plea of guilty the adolescent would receive a hearing to determine if he had been legally sane at the time he committed the murders. If he was determined to have been insane, Jenkins would be sent to an institution and receive medical treatment; if not, he would be remanded to a state prison, probably for his lifetime.

The next month a jury heard the teenager's sanity case. Defense attorneys presented the argument that Jenkins was suffering from schizophrenia and paranoia, and that he had murdered his family to save them from a dangerous world.

The prosecution argued that the teenager had been angry and frustrated with his parents because they had placed him in a boarding school that he detested. In the end, the jury was persuaded by the prosecution's case and found that Jenkins had been sane at the time of the murders. In June 1997 Joshua Jenkins was sentenced to 112 years in a state prison. At the time of his sentencing, he was seventeen years old.

The Joshua Jenkins case is a clear example of the difficulties of determining the role of a psychological disorder in the commission of a violent crime by an adolescent. In Jenkins's case, there was no disagreement among behaviorists that the teenager was mentally ill. The issue in the case became one of legal culpability—whether or not the adolescent was *legally* sane at the time of his crime. This is an area of continuing uncertainty and dispute among officers of the court, medical experts, and behaviorists. However, it is also an issue that is typically critical to the application of fair justice.

The diagnosis of mental illness and the assessment of its possible impact in a violent crime is not yet a precise science. In fact, it is often at odds with the legal view of sanity. In the case of Joshua Jenkins, as in those of many other violent adolescents, it is not yet possible to create a formula that balances the need for legal sanctions against the impact of a psychological disorder in a violent crime—and it may never be so. Beyond this, the brutality of many adolescent crimes, such as those committed by Jenkins, outrages the public and impels prosecutors to seek the maximum punishment the law will allow. However, in many cases of teenage murder, we are never able to determine satisfactorily *why* the murder was committed, even if we are able to attain some legal satisfaction for the crime. This was certainly true in the case of Joshua Jenkins.

Sadly, we do not understand why some adolescents murder their family members or close friends, apparently without anything close to a reasonable motive. Certainly, we have come to recognize the rage and urge for retribution that can overwhelm many teenagers, even though these strong emotions seem to be so foreign and troubling to most adults. However, if we reach back into our own recollections of adolescence, many of us will discover the shadowy traces of angry memories that we experienced. From the dimming perspective of advancing years, these feelings of rage and frustration seem insignificant and almost laughable. They seem like a "phase" in our life that was inevitable, perhaps unsettling, but one to be expected and passed through. We have forgotten the gnawing intensity of our own adolescent years, which were frequently filled with high-pitched emotions, unreasonable fears, unrealistic expectations, extremes of emotion, and a pervasive sense of isolation from the older generation around us.

Many of us were angry adolescents; however, most of us were not violent. Today, when we learn of an adolescent who inexplicably and brutally takes another life, we react with a sense of horror and perhaps anger. In part, this is because we have lost the essential memory of the teenage rage that may have been a fundamental part of our own lives. We cannot clearly recollect that phase in our growth process, which for the vast majority of us resulted in nothing more harmful than typical youthful pranks and misadventures. Today, these misadventures have been transformed into comic or educational fables that we often serve to our own children at appropriate moments. Such is the nature of our selective memories. Such is the way we have distanced ourselves from the potential violence of our past.

However, for some individuals, adolescent rage overpowers all else in their lives and impels them to a moment of explosive violence that is beyond our understanding and theirs. It is true that as adults many of us are successful survivors of our own adolescent rage and incessant need for retribution. If we wish to be honest, we must recognize that we are the fortunate ones. We are the individuals who have managed to escape from a dark, destructive byway on the path to adulthood, a byway that lies in wait for all adolescents in our society.

If we explore our deep and personal memories with truthfulness, care, and understanding, we are inevitably faced with several disturbing questions. Are we really so different from those "good kids" who murdered without reason? Or are we the lucky survivors of similar, now forgotten, emotions? Were we *really* such good kids, or were we simply the fortunate ones?

NOTES

1. "Boy Held in 3 Deaths—Mom Knifed, Classmates Shot," *San Francisco Chronicle*, 2 October 1997, A3.

2. Susan Howlett, "Days of Rage," *Los Angeles Times* (Internet Edition), 12 March 1996.

3. Ibid.

4. Ibid.

5. Ibid.

6. Emily Benedek, "A Death in the Family," *Redbook* (Internet Edition), 1 August 1994.

7. Susan Howlett, "Days of Rage," *Los Angeles Times* (Internet Edition), 12 March 1996.

8. Lorenza Munos and Antonio Olivo, "Mother's Slaying Baffles Neighbors," *Los Angeles Times Orange County Edition* (Internet Edition), 24 February 1996.

9. Ibid.

10. Ken Ellingwood, "Boy May Be Tried As Adult in Death of His Mother," *Los Angeles Times Orange County Edition* (Internet Edition), 27 February 1996.

11. Antonio Olivo and Ken Ellingwood, "A Family Torn from Within," *Los Angeles Times Home Edition* (Internet Edition), 29 May 1996.

12. Munos and Olivo.

13. Olivo and Ellingwood.

14. Ibid.

15. Ibid.

16. Ibid.

17. Ibid.

18. Dexter Filkins, "Father Mourns Wife's Death, Son's Future," *Los Angeles Times Orange County Edition* (Internet Edition), 3 March 1996.

19. Olivo and Ellingwood.

20. Munos and Olivo.

21. Ellingwood.

22. Thao Hua, "Youth in Murder Case Won't Be Tried As Adult," *Los Angeles Times Orange County Edition* (Internet Edition), 27 June 1996.

23. Ibid.

24. Ibid.

25. Ralph Ellis, "Teen Killed His Parents to Get Free," *Atlanta Journal and Constitution* (Internet Edition), 13 October 1995.

26. Ralph Ellis, "Teen Pleads Guilty to Slaying Parents," *Atlanta Journal and Constitution* (Internet Edition), 9 November 1995.

27. Ralph Ellis, "Youth Gets Consecutive Life Terms Plus 10 Years for Killing Parents," *Atlanta Journal and Constitution* (Internet Edition), 3 November 1995.

28. Ibid.

29. Ibid.

30. Benjamin G. Barlow, "Council Asked to Fund Search of Landfill," *Ahwatukee Foothills News* (Internet Edition), 6 March 1996.

31. Tom Brecke, "Bach to Be Tried As Adult in Classmate's Death," *Ahwatukee Foothills News* (Internet Edition), 8 May 1996.

32. Ibid.

33. American Psychiatric Association, *Diagnostic and Statistical Manual of Mental Disorders,* 4th ed. Washington, DC (1994), 645.

34. Ibid., 650.

35. Tony Perry, "D.A. Seeks to Try Boy, 15, As Adult in 5 Slayings," *Los Angeles Times Orange County Edition* (Internet Edition), 6 February 1996, Part A, 3.

4

SENSELESS ACTS
OF VIOLENCE

In violence we forget who we are.

Mary McCarthy
On the Contrary

Shawn Graves was a husky, pleasant sixteen-year-old who had a natural penchant for athletics. Even as a freshman in high school he had earned a position as a defensive tackle on the school football team, and he would often be in the starting lineup for important games. Now, as a sophomore, he was considered a valuable member of the team and was widely recognized as a likeable, popular classmate. As a student, Shawn was average but hardworking. He had no criminal record and no history of violence. Shawn did not use drugs or alcohol, nor was he affiliated with a gang.

On the evening of January 2, 1997, Graves and a friend decided to drive to a nearby county to visit a mutual friend. Shawn borrowed his grandmother's car. As was his habit, the teenager had not been drinking or using drugs. However, for some reason, Shawn's friend brought a handgun along on the journey. Graves and his friend drove to their destination, visited for a time with their friend, and then Shawn drove his companion home. However, Shawn's friend left his 9-mm automatic handgun behind in the car. Police would later learn that the weapon had been stolen.

At 2:49 the next morning, Walton County Deputy Henry Huff stopped Graves, who had left his friend's house, clocking him at speeds as high as eighty-eight miles per hour. As the deputy exited his patrol car to approach Shawn's vehicle, he routinely turned on the video camera mounted on the dash. Shortly after Huff approached the teenager's vehicle, Graves inexplicably grabbed the handgun from the seat next to him and fired two shots, point-blank, into the deputy's chest. Fortunately, Huff was wearing a protective vest at the time. The entire incident was captured on videotape.

Immediately after firing at the officer, the teenager fled the scene at high speed. Huff, who was uninjured, radioed for help, and a police chase ensued. Twelve miles away other officers apprehended Graves when he wrecked his grandmother's vehicle and was unable to drive farther. The teenager climbed out of the damaged vehicle still holding the 9-mm weapon in his hand and faced the surrounding officers. Fortunately, they acted with great restraint, and the teenager was taken into custody without incident. He was subsequently charged with aggravated assault on a police officer, theft by receiving and taking, possession of a pistol by a minor, and attempting to elude an officer.

Shawn Graves was remanded to the adult court system rather than juvenile court, because he had attacked a police

---

Snapshot Profile of Shawn Graves

A sixteen-year-old high school student, a star athlete and universally recognized as a stable, happy individual. Graves had no history of violence or a criminal record. After being stopped by an officer for speeding, the teenager fired two shots, point-blank, into the officer's chest with a handgun that had been left behind by a friend. The officer was wearing a protective vest at the time and was uninjured. Graves was arrested and eventually pleaded guilty to the charges against him under a plea bargaining arrangement. He was sentenced to twelve years' imprisonment.

officer with a possible intent to murder. All who knew Shawn, including members of the prosecution team, were completely shocked at his sudden, inexplicable outburst of violence. The teenager had no history of criminal behavior, came from a respected, close-knit, middle-class family, and was considered an easy-going, quiet, and friendly individual. He was indisputably one of the "good kids."

Three months after the incident, Shawn Graves was sentenced to twelve years in prison under a plea bargain agreement with the district attorney. The only explanation that the teenager was ever able to give for his actions was that he had acted in a moment of panic. Sadly, that inexplicable moment of senseless violence could cost Shawn Graves as many as twelve years of his life.

THE INEXPLICABLE

How do we explain the actions of an adolescent like Shawn Graves? Even if we are able to approach an understanding of the insidious emotional forces that drive a teenage mother to commit neonaticide or a teenage son to murder his parents, there are still a large number of good kids who commit violent acts without any rational motive. Like those teenagers driven by fear and denial, or rage and retribution, these violent juveniles act in a way that is wholly foreign to their backgrounds and family values. These are adolescents without a history of violence, often from close families or privileged backgrounds, who commit the most gruesome violent crimes without any apparent purpose or explanation.

It is extremely difficult, if not impossible, to comprehend such violence. In most cases the adolescents who commit these crimes provide only vague and diffuse reasons for their actions. These perpetrators often refer to feelings of fear, frustration, powerlessness, anger, or lack of control, feelings that are undefined and unfocused yet obviously pervasive. Sometimes these teenagers commit their crimes with the active participation of a friend or lover, who shares their same inexplicable compulsion for violence.

In some cases of random teenage violence and murder, the use of drugs or alcohol is involved, although this is certainly not always the situation. In a few instances there is clear evidence of physical or sexual abuse in the family environment, or signs of a debilitating psychological disorder. However, in many cases, like that of Shawn Graves, none of these conditions seems to exist.

Defense attorneys work diligently on behalf of their young clients, generally trying to summon understandable motivations from their childhood to explain their egregious crimes. However, in all but the most obvious cases it is difficult to find mitigating circumstances. Juries rarely find such reasons pertinent to the ultimate guilt of a teenage murderer. Moreover, these inexplicable acts of violence and murder are frequently brazen, callous, and extraordinarily vicious, producing an understandable fear and outrage in the public and members of a jury. Under these circumstances, the already inexplicable nature of the crime becomes virtually beyond understanding for most individuals.

If it is difficult for adults to comprehend the essential nature of teenage rage that leads to murder, it is nearly impossible to grasp the fundamental reason why some adolescents kill in the absence of such an obvious emotional force. In many of these murders there is an apparent element of random, wanton violence that seems to explode without warning, reason, or purpose. It is as if the teenager is driven to commit the most brutal acts imaginable, and the identity of the victim is an unimportant, coincidental aspect in the case. These crimes are arguably the most disturbing of all adolescent violence, because they are so explosive, unanticipated, and threatening to the foundations of our society.

Sadly, these crimes are becoming more frequent in America as we continue to experience a general increase in the rate of murder of individuals unknown and unrelated to their attackers. Certainly, as a society we have failed in our efforts to understand this kind of random, senseless violence at most levels. If we are to make any headway in combatting this kind of crime in the future, perhaps our efforts should begin with an understanding of why our own children resort to this extreme and senseless form of violence.

THRILL KILLINGS

In January 1994, John and Reta Jarvis answered a ring at the front door of their quiet home in Whitehead, Nova Scotia, and were greeted by a shotgun blast. John Jarvis was killed instantly, and his wife was seriously wounded, partially paralyzed in her head and face. The attacker was their thirteen-year-old neighbor, who had no history of violence or encounters with the law. When the teenager was asked in court why he had committed such an incredible crime, he casually explained that he was angry because his father had refused to buy him some chewing tobacco. According to his testimony, he had decided two minutes before he pulled the trigger that he would shoot the first person in the neighborhood who happened to answer his ring at their door, so he would know what it was like to take a life.

Frank Troope was an aging Anglican priest who lived with his wife, Jocelyn, in a pleasant suburban area of Montreal, Canada. Troope and his wife were seventy-five years old, clearly devoted to each other, and widely considered to be loving, caring, and gentle individuals. They were also an important part of their community and widely respected by all who knew them. In 1995, Frank and Jocelyn Troope were found brutally bludgeoned to death in their home. They had both been murdered with a baseball bat in an especially gruesome attack that had not been prompted by theft or robbery. When the perpetrators of this shocking crime were arrested, they turned out to be a trio of juveniles, all of whom came from affluent, stable family environments. Their ages were thirteen, fourteen, and fifteen years.

A seasoned Montreal detective who worked on the Troope case described the boys' motives this way: "It [the murders] was completely senseless. I've never seen such a merciless killing."[1] As the investigation came to a conclusion, it was learned that the juveniles had murdered the priest and his wife merely "for the kick of it."[2] The evening before the trio committed their crime, they had met to discuss how they could find someone to kill—anyone. Frank and Jocelyn Troope were selected without any apparent reason other than the ease with which they could be attacked—an essential element that often defines the gruesome crime of thrill killing.

These are only two of many cases of senseless thrill killings that have been committed by teenagers in recent years. Homicides of this type are extraordinarily brutal and shocking, because they claim victims for no apparent purpose other than the excitement and pleasure it generates for the murderer. However, thrill killings are not something new to North American society. In fact, this kind of purposeless crime has been with us for many decades.

In 1959, actors Dean Stockwell and Bradford Dillman portrayed two teenage thrill killers in the movie *Compulsion*, directed by Richard Fleisher. This dark, compelling production was based on the notorious 1924 murder case of Nathan Leopold and Richard Loeb, who were the real-life killers of a young boy—a victim selected essentially at random because he would be incapable of defending himself. In *Compulsion*, Fleisher examines the senseless murder plot that was hatched and carried out by two brilliant but bored teenage perpetrators. A good deal of the production focuses on the uneven, unhealthy relationship that developed between a dominant, ego-driven, and apparently heartless adolescent and his passive, insecure, and easily manipulated best friend. The result of this bizarre and troubled relationship was the murder of an innocent boy simply for the experience of committing the crime. This movie was the first of its kind to closely examine the subject of thrill killing, along with the twisted and intricate relationship that existed between the perpetrators.

Although *Compulsion* may seem outdated by the standards of the late twentieth century, the intense character study of the Leopold and Loeb characters is as fascinating and enlightening today as it was forty years ago. These intelligent but emotionally devastated adolescents decided to murder for no reason other than to experience the extreme emotion and sense of superiority to be derived from what they believed would be the perfect crime. They were prototypical thrill killers in a time seemingly far removed from our own but contemporary in terms of their heinous and familiar motivation.

In 1994, nearly forty years after *Compulsion* was released, director Oliver Stone brought *Natural Born Killers* to theaters across America, once again examining the personalities and crimes of thrill killers. However, unlike the cerebral and pedantic murderers in *Compulsion*, Stone's primary characters are a young couple who thrive on the very concept of senseless murder. Mickey and Mallory Knox are fugitive lovers who murder for the sense of power and retribution they derive from the act, without any hint of regard for their victims. They are anything but murderers with a plan and purpose; rather, they are compelled to kill purely for pleasure of the act itself.

During the first half of Stone's movie, Mickey and Mallory Knox murder in excess of fifty victims. Throughout their killing spree it becomes disturbingly obvious to the viewer that the Knoxes are beyond any understandable motive for their violent actions. They are simply and completely thrill killers. Whereas the characters in *Compulsion* derive a sense of superiority through the careful planning and execution of their crime, the murderers in *Natural Born Killers* seek only the sense of domination that they derive from the most gruesome, callous, and random violence they are able to perpetrate. However, in both movies, the murderous lead characters share the same primary motivation—to kill solely for the perceived thrill of the act.

How accurate are the portrayals of such characters in *Compulsion* and *Natural Born Killers*? Are the exploits of these young murderers related in any way to the growing number of crimes that are committed each year by American thrill killers? The answers to these questions depend on how one chooses to view these classic films. As to specifics, one production takes liberties with the facts of the case, and the other is (thankfully) fiction. However, at a deeper level, both movies offer us a valid and accurate glimpse into the dark and troubling motivations of teenage thrill killers. In the four murderers examined in these two productions, it is fairly easy to identify many characteristics and behavior patterns that are shared by contemporary adolescent thrill killers. Among these similarities are the apparent presence of emotional or personality disorders, boredom, generalized rage, a burning desire for retribution against society, a compulsion for the domination of others, low self-esteem hidden beneath a false sense of superiority, and many of the qualities of a classic sociopath. In fact, at the root of their drives and motivations there is little difference between the intellectualization of murder as portrayed by the Leopold-Loeb characters, the wanton physical violence of Mickey and Mallory Knox, and today's adolescent thrill killers. Each of these characters, fictional or not, embodies the same compulsion for random murder that we find in contemporary thrill-killing teenagers. Most troubling is that we have yet to come to a consensus about why our society so often spawns teenage thrill killers. This category of crime and its perpetrator remain largely enigmatic, often beyond our understanding, and always horrifying.

In late 1997, Todd Rizzo, an eighteen-year-old from Connecticut, worked at a video store in his hometown. He seemed to live a quiet, ordinary life. He had recently been discharged from the military after nine months service and had no history of violence or criminal activities. While working at the video store, Rizzo came to know a number of regular customers. Among them was thirteen-year-old Stanley Edwards, who would sometimes ride his bicycle to the video store, where he was helped by the older teenager.

On September 30, 1997, Edwards was riding his bike home and happened to pass by Rizzo's residence. The older teenager was standing in front of his house at the time, and Edwards stopped to chat with him. Rizzo invited the boy into the area behind his home to hunt for snakes. Excited to receive attention from the older teenager, Edwards quickly agreed and went with Rizzo to the rear of the home. However, he did not see Rizzo hide a ten-inch, three-pound sledgehammer underneath his garments.

For a few moments, the pair worked their way around Rizzo's backyard with a flashlight, hunting for snakes. However, when Edwards was not looking, the older teenager withdrew the sledgehammer from underneath his clothes and hit the boy on the side of the head from behind. Then, according to Rizzo's later statements to police, "I sat on him like a horse and hit him a bunch of times in the head because I didn't want him to scream out and alert neighbors. I can't remember how many times I hit him, but he made a gurgling sound again. So I hit him at least one or two more times."[3] After murdering Edwards, Rizzo dumped his body a few miles away from the scene of the crime. However, the boy's remains were soon discovered, and a local witness linked Rizzo to the dumpsite. When the teenager was interrogated about the details of the

---

Snapshot Profile of Todd Rizzo

An eighteen-year-old recently discharged from the military, who had no history of violence or criminal record. After meeting a thirteen-year-old at the video store where he worked, Rizzo lured the boy into the backyard of his home and bludgeoned him to death with a sledgehammer. His only stated motivation for the murder was to experience the thrill of the crime.

crime, he offered this incredible motive to investigators: "I decided I wanted to try and kill him [Edwards] for no good reason and get away with it. It was like a sort of urge, I guess."[4]

The crime committed by Todd Rizzo is not unique, but it is also not the most common form of thrill killing. Most of these crimes that are committed by teenagers involve two or more perpetrators acting together, not an individual acting alone. When two perpetrators are involved in murder (the most common scenario), one of the adolescents is usually dominant and the other easily manipulated or led, as portrayed so many years ago in *Compulsion*. However, even when the number of perpetrators exceeds two, there is typically evidence of a single, dominant personality in the group who dictates the criminal behavior of the other, more passive members. In some cases an older, more criminally sophisticated adolescent who is able to successfully manipulate a previously nonviolent individual will lead the partnership or group in a random act of murder.

In some instances, two or more teenagers will commit a thrill killing without any individual history of violent behavior among them. When this situation occurs, the facts of the case often lead us to believe that the perpetrators may not have committed such a brutal crime on their own, as individuals. However, there frequently develops a dark synergy, one that is seen over and over again in cases of teenage thrill killers who operate in partnership—a kind of magnification and explosion of latent violence that would not be possible had it not been for the partnership.

In 1997, two horrific incidents of thrill killing took place on the opposite coasts of our country. In both cases the homicides were allegedly committed by a pair of teenagers with no previous history of violence. Both crimes involved senseless murders in which the victims became the unfortunate targets of teenagers intent on experiencing the emotion of randomly taking a life.

In a Rut

On January 5, 1997, the worst case of homicide in the history of Bellevue, Washington, was formally opened for investigation. On that chilling Sunday, law enforcement officers learned that an entire family had been brutally slain sometime after midnight of the previous day. Dead were William Wilson, 52, his wife, Rose Wilson, 46, and their daughters Julia, 17, and Kimberly, 20. William, Rose, and Julia's bodies had been discovered in their home, where they had each been brutally beaten on the head with a blunt object and stabbed in the neck. Mr. and Mrs. Wilson had died in their bedroom, while Julia had been killed in a hallway.

Kimberly's body had been discovered in a neighborhood park several blocks from the Wilson residence. She had been severely beaten and strangled to death. From an investigation of the park crime scene, officials soon determined that Kimberly had been attacked in the early morning hours of January 4, some time before the remaining members of her family were slain. After her murder, the attackers went to the Wilson home and bludgeoned and stabbed her parents and younger sister, probably to eliminate anyone who would have known Kimberly's whereabouts or with whom she had been meeting that morning.

Four days after the discovery of the Wilson family, investigators arrested seventeen-year-old Alex Baranyi on suspicion of murder. Police had learned that Baranyi had arranged to meet Kimberly Wilson on the night of her murder and was probably the last person to see her alive. Pursuing their suspicions, investigators discovered the Wilson family's telephone, CD player, and VCR in the teenager's room.

When the announcement of Baranyi's arrest was made, members of the press immediately speculated about the existence of other suspects in the case, given the number of victims discovered at the Wilson home and the gruesome nature of the crime scene. However, officials steadfastly refused to provide details of the murders or discuss the possibility of other suspects.

On January 14, 1997, Alex Baranyi was formally charged with four counts of aggravated first-degree murder. According to court records filed at that time, the teenager had told investigators that he had planned to murder someone because he was "in a rut."[5] In effect, Baranyi openly proclaimed himself to be a thrill killer of four innocent victims. There was no mention made in the court records of an accomplice in the crime.

Alex Baranyi was an enigmatic and strange figure, who initially seemed an unlikely individual to commit such gruesome crimes. He had no history of significant violence, although he did have a brush with legal authorities the year before the Wilson family murders. In April 1996, a teenage girl had telephoned Bellevue police to report that Baranyi had threatened to kill her and had hit her hard enough to cause a concussion. The teenager swore out a complaint against Baranyi, but no formal action was ever taken; the investigation was eventually dropped when police decided that the altercation was a "mutual combat" situation.[6] The notations in the case file indicated that the incident was determined to be teenage horseplay that had escalated into a physical altercation, with both parties suffering minor injuries. Other than this citizen complaint, the alleged murderer of the Wilson family had had no contact with law enforcement personnel.

The same day that Alex Baranyi was formally charged with murder, residents of Bellevue learned that his best friend, David C. Anderson, seventeen years old, had also been arrested on charges of murder in the Wilson case. Court documents related to Baranyi's charges had led the press and public to believe that the teenager had acted alone in the crime, so the announcement of a second arrest came as somewhat of a surprise. However, as matters developed, it seemed inevitable that Anderson would be implicated in the violence that investigators were certain began with Alex Baranyi.

Baranyi's alleged accomplice was a native of the Woodridge area of Bellevue who had once lived within blocks of where Kimberly Wilson was murdered. He had also been Baranyi's closest friend for many years. However, like his best friend, Anderson had no previous criminal record and no documented history of violence before he was arrested for murder.

Immediately after bringing formal charges against Baranyi and arresting Anderson, investigators suggested to the press that the two teenagers had planned to murder the Wilson family for some time and had even discussed the contemplated crime with their mutual friends. This information was quickly denied by other sources, and the true motive for the murders became a point of intense speculation in the press. To compound the uncertainty and confusion that surrounded the crime, police were initially unable or unwilling to disclose Anderson's precise role in the killings, or even if he had been inside the Wilson home at the time of the attack.

Two weeks after the arrests of Baranyi and Anderson, prosecutors clarified many of these uncertainties. They announced that the two teenagers had prepared a list of potential murder victims and together had acted on their plans by killing the Wilson family. Prosecutors were now convinced that the two teenagers had methodically planned and carried out murder solely for the sheer excitement of the crime.

High on the list of potential victims prepared by Baranyi and Anderson was Kimberly Wilson. Prosecutors disclosed that Anderson had apparently bragged for a year to friends and acquaintances that he planned to kill Kimberly, although there seemed to be no specific reason for her selection as a victim. On at least one occasion Anderson had displayed a baseball bat and several knives that he claimed he would use to carry out the murders. Investigators had already determined that one or more knives and a baseball bat had probably been used against the Wilsons, although no murder weapons had been recovered. However, Anderson's bragging to his friends now became strong evidence of premeditation.

Prosecutors believed that Anderson had beaten Kimberly Wilson while Baranyi restrained and strangled her, in the neighborhood park near her home. Realizing that the Wilson family probably knew who Kimberly was meeting that night, the pair then went to the Wilson home, where they jointly murdered the remaining family members. Although Baranyi had refused to name Anderson as his accomplice in the murders, he had admitted to investigators that another individual had beaten Kimberly and later accompanied him to the Wilson home to murder the other family members. During this interrogation, Baranyi had also admitted that Anderson was his closest friend. From these statements investigators were quickly able to piece together the most likely scenario for the brutal crime spree.

Physical and forensic evidence at the scene of the Wilson murders strongly implicated both teenagers in the crime. Investigators found two different sets of bloody footprints at the scene, which reportedly matched those of Baranyi and Anderson. They also discovered a piece of a black T-shirt that matched a piece of fabric found in the vehicle Anderson drove on the night of the murders. Lengths of rope used to strangle Kimberly Wilson were also linked to the teenagers. Nonetheless, and despite earlier statements by Alex Baranyi that had implicated both teenagers in the murders, the two suspects claimed that on the night of the murders they had been together playing video games and not in the vicinity of either crime scene. However, two days after they offered this alibi, one of the teenagers contradicted it and claimed that he had actually been alone at the time of the slayings.

The murders of the Wilson family spawned intense headlines in this traditionally peaceful area of Washington. Reporters began digging into the past of the two teenage suspects, searching for some clue to their motivations. However, as is the case in so many incidents of thrill killing, there was little sense to be made of the crime or the perpetrators.

Alex Kevin Baranyi had been born in Pennsylvania in 1979, the only child of Patricia and Alex Joseph Baranyi.

When Alex was still a child, the family had moved to the state of Washington. In 1987 the Baranyi marriage collapsed, and Alex was sent to live with his father, although both parents retained legal custody of the boy. Two years later, Baranyi's father left his job as a computer consultant and moved back to Pennsylvania. For a few months Alex stayed on in Washington with his mother, but he was later moved to his father's house.

By the middle of 1989 Alex Baranyi's father was back in Washington, and Alex was once more living with his mother. By the fall of that year, Alex had again been shuffled back to his father. By this time, Alex's mother was growing concerned that the repeated displacement of her son between herself and her ex-husband was unhealthy for the boy. However, no formal restructuring of the custody arrangements was ever made.

Alex, his father, and his stepmother eventually moved to Bellevue, Washington, from where Alex would visit his mother each month. However, in the summer of 1996, Alex once again moved away from his father's house, this time into the home of a sixteen-year-old friend, Bob Boyd, where he paid $50 each month for a room. During part of the time that Baranyi was renting a room from the Boyd family, David Anderson also lived in the house. It was at this time, while Baranyi and Anderson were living with the Boyds, that Anderson introduced Baranyi to Kimberly Wilson.

Snapshot Profiles of Alex Baranyi and David Anderson

Two seventeen-year-old best friends who had no histories of significant violence or criminal activities. Both adolescents were deeply involved in a "gothic" lifestyle that heavily influenced their behavior. Baranyi and Anderson combined to murder an entire family of four in Bellevue, Washington, but were unable to express a motive for their crimes more meaningful than merely the excitement of killing.

Kimberly Ann Wilson, the eldest daughter of William and Rose Wilson, had graduated from Bellevue High School in 1995. Awaiting her reporting date to join the AmeriCorps program in San Diego, California, she had been living with her parents, working in a local retail store, and attending classes at Bellevue Community College. Unlike the quiet, withdrawn, and secretive Baranyi, Kimberly Wilson was vivacious, outgoing, opinionated, and had many friends. She was an avid fan of the movies and hoped someday to become an actress. When Kimberly was first introduced to Baranyi it seemed clear to those who knew the pair that she had little in common with him. However, after their initial meeting they did see each other from time to time.

David Anderson was a native of Bellevue who had been raised very near the park where Kimberly Wilson was murdered. In 1989 the Baranyi and Anderson families lived two blocks apart, and the boys had become best friends. Neighbors and acquaintances recalled that the two had been inseparable and even dressed alike, although there were periods when the pair had disagreements and would part for a time. Of the two teenagers, David Anderson was the more outgoing, while Baranyi seemed frequently sullen and withdrawn. Anderson was also known as a proficient wrestler, and like his best friend had been interested in fantasy, role-playing games.

Baranyi, Anderson, and several of their acquaintances were deeply involved in a fantasy-driven lifestyle known as "gothic," which involved extensive role playing, late-night meetings, and the collection and use of unusual weapons, such as swords and unique knives. Members of this loose association would gather on weekend nights to play a variety of fantasy roles that involved medieval themes, vampirism, and legendary conflicts between historical figures. At one point Baranyi and Anderson joined an organization known as the Dark Ballad Gaming Society, which brought together aficionados of the gothic lifestyle in a more structured way than did their usual impromptu gatherings. However, Baranyi, Anderson, and their friends were soon accused of taking their roles too seriously for the comfort of the other members, and they were asked to leave the society. According to one member who was later interviewed by the press, "They [Baranyi and his friends] lost track of pulling off the mask and getting back to reality."[7] However, despite their ejection from the Dark Ballad Gaming Society, there was no evidence of physical violence reported to authorities.

Two years before Baranyi was barred from the Dark Ballad Gaming Society, he had been dropped from a similar group because he had touched another member, breaking one of the most fundamental rules of the organization. In both groups, fellow members apparently concluded that Baranyi and Anderson had difficulty controlling their behavior during their fantasy encounters.

According to Baranyi's former roommate, the teenager had a collection of unusual weapons and was clearly obsessed with the gothic lifestyle. He was also an ardent fan of the television series *The Highlander* and often played out a similar fantasy role in his personal life. According to Bob Boyd: "He's a sword collector. He's really, really big into swords. He talks about Highlanders all the time."[8] What role the gothic lifestyle played in the gruesome murders committed by Alex Baranyi and David Anderson remains unknown. However, it is clear that both teenagers had been heavily influenced by this unusual fantasy avocation. Given the nature of the Wilson family murders and the weapons apparently used in the crime, it cannot be ruled out that the gothic fantasies that had been so much a part of these adolescents' lives may have overwhelmed them at a crucial moment.

In 1994, Washington passed a law that required juveniles over the age of fifteen to be tried as adults for all serious violent crimes. At that time, a law was already in existence that prohibited prosecutors from seeking the death penalty for anyone under the age of eighteen. Since Baranyi and Anderson were under eighteen years old when they allegedly murdered the Wilson family, the teenagers will be automatically tried as adults. However, if they are found guilty, neither will be eligible for the death penalty.

One of the striking and troubling aspects to this case of thrill killing is the intense and uneasy relationship that existed between the teenagers charged with murdering four victims. From the facts of the case, it seems inevitable that a comparison could be made with the Leopold-Loeb relationship referred to in the movie *Compulsion*. However, the question that remains unanswered in the Baranyi-Anderson case is, which of the pair was the dominant force that led these teenagers to murder for the sheer thrill of the act? Was it the sullen, withdrawn dreamer, or his outgoing, talkative best friend?

A Horrible Murder in Central Park

On May 28, 1997, two fifteen-year-olds made separate appearances in Manhattan Criminal Court to answer charges of an especially horrific murder that had seized both local and national headlines. Daphne Abdela and Christopher Vasquez, both looking even younger than their years, were accused of the brutal slashing murder of a forty-four-year-old real estate broker, Michael McMorrow, in New York's Central Park. By all accounts this crime had been among the most vicious single homicides committed by a New York teenager in recent memory.

The victim's body had been discovered early in the morning on May 23, 1997, in Central Park Lake at the crossroads of Strawberry Fields and 72nd Street. McMorrow's throat had been slashed, and he had received dozens of stab wounds to his neck, face, chest, stomach, and wrists. According to one investigator on the case, the condition of the victim's body was horrific: "It was an extremely vicious crime. It was one of the worst things I've ever seen."[9] After the brutal murder McMorrow had been robbed of the contents of his wallet and his identification had been destroyed, although it was thought from the first that this had most likely not been a homicide committed in the course of a robbery.

At their first court appearance the unlikely teenage murderers stunned court observers with their obvious youth and apparent lack of concern for the overwhelming situation in which they found themselves. Vasquez was a bright, unassertive, former altar boy who, according to courtroom reporters, appeared no older than twelve as he stood before the court in rimless glasses and a "fade" haircut. The charges filed against him were second-degree murder and robbery. Daphne Abdela, the baby-faced, slightly pudgy daughter of a very wealthy and successful New York businessman, seemed equally child-like and distant from the gruesome crime for which she was to be tried. She was charged with the same crimes as her boyfriend of two months. Both teenagers were promptly ordered held without bail because of the heinous nature of the murder of McMorrow.

From the onset of the investigation, Daphne Abdela's attorney made it clear that the slaying of Michael McMorrow had been the sole work of Christopher Vasquez, and not his client. However, Abdela had already confessed to investigators that she had been with Vasquez during the murder and had ordered him to throw the body into the lake and to eviscerate it so that it would not float. According to police records, Abdela had said to interrogators, "I told Chris to gut the body—it will sink because he's a fatty."[10]

As the press and public would learn several months after the crime, Abdela had also made a number of other incriminating statements to investigators that seemed to indicate a much deeper involvement in the murder than one of a passive witness. On the other hand, Christopher Vasquez remained steadfastly silent about his role in the crime, and his attorney consistently refused to release any information to the press, reiterating his position that the details of the crime should be first heard at his client's trial.

The victim, Michael McMorrow, had been an enigmatic

man, although he had been generally regarded as nonviolent and likeable. A few individuals who knew him claimed that McMorrow was an alcoholic, who spent virtually every evening drunk in Central Park. However most of McMorrow's friends knew a much different person. According to one of his coworkers who had known him for several years, McMorrow had been "the hardest-working, most honest real estate agent I've ever met."[11] It had been McMorrow's invariable habit to work seven days a week, always paying close attention to his job responsibilities and his clients. A bachelor, he was described by most coworkers as a kindhearted, caring, but somewhat isolated figure.

Like his friends and acquaintances, McMorrow's family could not come to an understanding why such an apparently gentle, outgoing man should be so brutally slain. Although he was recognized as a somewhat lonely individual, McMorrow had been also considered to be a gregarious, open man, and an excellent performer on the job. If he had any flaw at all it was that he drank a bit too much beer, although those who knew him well did not consider this to be a significant foible.

Despite his generally solid reputation, McMorrow did have at least one curious habit, which was probably the result of his lonely lifestyle. Each evening after leaving his real estate office on the Upper West Side of New York, McMorrow would walk to a local supermarket and purchase beer. From there he would stroll across Central Park, leisurely drinking the beer he had bought. Since he lived with his eighty-year-old mother, Margaret, McMorrow was rarely in a hurry to return home from work and would sometimes join friends for a few hours of chatting and drinking beer on a favorite Central Park bench. Occasionally, according to one friend of McMorrow's, he would indulge himself by smoking a joint of marijuana and entertaining his companions with impersonations of film stars like Kirk Douglas. However, on most evenings, McMorrow would spend his time alone in the park, alternatively strolling, sitting on a park bench, and enjoying his beer.

Around six o'clock on the evening of his murder, McMorrow had walked to Central Park as usual, carrying with him two or three large cans of Guinness beer. A few hours later he happened to meet Daphne Abdela and Christopher Vasquez in the Strawberry Fields area of the park. McMorrow had known Abdela from their mutual attendance at a drug rehabilitation program several months previously.

Sometime around midnight, McMorrow, Vasquez, and Abdela walked together to a gazebo near the Central Park Lake. An hour later a nearby witness heard a man scream repeatedly for help—it was Michael McMorrow. According to Daphne Abdela's subsequent statements to police, Vasquez and McMorrow became involved in an altercation that resulted in the victim being stabbed dozens of times and his throat slit. At the time of the murder, all three individuals had been drinking beer, but none had apparently been using drugs.

The witness who heard the attack on McMorrow was a police officer who happened to be on a routine foot patrol through Central Park. The officer investigated the area but found no immediate evidence of a crime and did not discover McMorrow's body, which by then had been pitched into the lake by his attackers. However, the policeman was later able to identify Abdela and Vasquez as the two teenagers who left the area of the murder shortly after the victim's screams subsided.

Snapshot Profiles of Daphne Abdela and Christopher Vasquez

Two very bright fifteen-year-olds, each raised in stable but economically different family environments. As boyfriend and girlfriend, they are accused of murdering a forty-four-year-old man by stabbing him dozens of times, slitting his throat, mutilating his body, and throwing it into a lake in Central Park. The motive for the crime is uncertain, although it is likely to have been a thrill killing.

At approximately the same time that McMorrow was being murdered, Daphne Abdela's father placed a telephone call to police to report her missing. He had become concerned when she had not returned home at such a late hour, and he had no idea where his daughter could be. When police officers arrived at the Abdela residence to follow up on the telephone call they found Daphne and Christopher in a utility room, washing blood from their hands and clothes. However, the officers were not yet aware of Michael McMorrow's murder and had no reason to suspect these unlikely looking adolescents of homicide. When officers questioned Abdela and Vasquez about the blood on their hands and clothes, the teenagers told them that they had fallen while rollerblading in Central Park. Apparently satisfied with the explanation, the officers left the Abdela residence without taking any further action.

Less than an hour later, an anonymous emergency telephone call was made to police by a young female. She reported that a friend of hers had jumped into the Central Park Lake and disappeared. Police traced this call and discovered that it had come from the Abdela residence. Once again, investigators called on Daphne Abdela. When confronted with the details of the anonymous telephone call, the teenager admitted that she had placed it.

According to investigators, Abdela initially seemed to be in a state of hysteria. However, the officers quickly came to the conclusion that she was feigning her emotional state and pressed her for more information about the telephone call. It was then that Abdela finally described the gruesome murder of Michael McMorrow and blamed the crime on her boyfriend, Christopher Vasquez. After disclosing the details of the homicide, Abdela led police to the crime scene at Central Park Lake, where the horribly slashed body of Michael McMorrow was recovered.

From the beginning, investigators and prosecutors were confronted with a crime that had no apparent motive. To compound the uncertainty and confusion in the case, Daphne Abdela had been argumentative with interrogators, giving information that was sometimes conflicting. On the other hand, Christopher Vasquez said very little to authorities, making any understanding of his actions even more problematic. What became immediately obvious to the press and the public was that these two fifteen-year-olds were very unlikely murderers, even though it was clear that both were deeply involved in a senseless and atrocious thrill killing.

Christopher Vasquez was the son of a working-class family that lived in a modest area of New York's Upper East Side. Two years before the McMorrow murder, his parents had separated, which apparently signaled for him the beginning of a period of depression and anger that had previously not been typical of the teenager. Vasquez had no documented history of violence and no criminal record. Unlike her boyfriend, Daphne Abdela came from an affluent background. She was the adopted, only child of a wealthy executive and a French-born model, who enjoyed a comfortable lifestyle in an exclusive apartment building on Central Park West. However, those who knew the teenager described her as often sullen, angry, and unhappy, despite her privileged background.

Both Abdela and Vasquez were exceptionally bright teenagers. Vasquez attended an elite private school on a scholarship, while Abdela was enrolled in the prestigious Loyola School, run by Jesuit priests. However, despite their intellectual affinity, the personalities of the two teenagers were very different. Christopher Vasquez was reticent and passive, while his girlfriend was often outspoken and abrasive. In fact, Abdela had been asked to leave two private schools because of her persistently argumentative, rebellious, and negative attitude. In addition, Abdela had a juvenile criminal record, which remained sealed by the state of New York because of her young age. Those who knew Christopher Vasquez consistently portrayed him as quiet, unassuming, and polite. He was described by one longtime neighbor this way: "He's not a trou-blemaker at all. Anytime you see him, he is with his grand-mother coming from shopping or coming back from school."[12]

Both teenagers shared a minor history of alcohol and drug use, although they were apparently not using drugs on the night of Michael McMorrow's murder. Vasquez had been treated with antidepressant medication since around the time of his parents' separation, two years before the murder. It has been reported in the press that both teenagers engaged in regular sessions of beer drinking in Central Park, where they may have come into contact with their victim on previous occasions.

Soon after the teenagers were arrested and charged with murder, their respective attorneys began to outline possible avenues of defense for their clients. Abdela's attorney took the position that his client had had no direct involvement in the crime and that it was her boyfriend who had committed the murder, alone and in a rage. Vasquez's attorney alluded to his client's two-year history of psychological problems and a dif-ficult family environment as possible contributing factors. Ac-cordingly, both teenagers pleaded not guilty to all the charges filed against them. However, from the prosecution's point of view, little of this was surprising or significant; prosecutors were convinced that both Abdela and Vasquez had actively participated in an act of homicide.

Despite the position taken by Daphne Abdela's attorney, several of his client's statements to police seemed to indicate a deeper involvement in the crime. Moreover, a few of Abdela's recorded comments demonstrate a brazen callousness and dis-regard for her actions that seem disturbingly reminiscent of others who have been involved in thrill killings. For example, as noted, Abdela had earlier admitted to police that she had or-dered Vasquez to eviscerate their victim so that his body would sink to the bottom of Central Park Lake. Later she had violently chastised her father for calling the police and involv-ing her in the crime: "Why'd you [expletive] call the cops? You got everybody involved. Where was I going to go? Of course I'd come home. What was I going to do? Sleep in the park with the dead body?"[13]

During her initial interviews with investigators, Abdela also made a misstatement that must have seemed very telling to prosecutors. While trying to explain her limited role in the attack on McMorrow, the teenager said: "Chris cut his throat while I was giving him CPR. Mike's my bud[dy]. I can't believe he's dead. When we killed him . . . No. No. I mean, Chris killed him. I tried to save him."

Although the nature of Daphne Abdela's involvement in the slaying of Michael McMorrow remains controversial, she pleaded guilty to manslaughter on March 11, 1998. A month later, she was sentenced to a minimum of three years in prison. Christopher Vasquez is still awaiting trial. It may be the case that we never fully learn the true roles of these teenagers in Michael McMorrow's thrill killing. In many ways, this seems an issue of limited importance to all but the defendants. It is the senseless and horrible way in which this likeable man died that overshadows all else about this crime.

Murder in a Casino

The molestation and murder of seven-year-old Sherrice Iverson in a Nevada casino in May 1997 shocked all who read accounts of this horrible crime. Not only was her homicide especially atrocious, but it was a random, senseless act of brutality that was allegedly carried out by an eighteen-year-old honor student who had met her only hours before the crime. To compound the troubling nature of this murder, the perpetrator has remained a shadowy, unknown adolescent, who seemed to most observers to be an unlikely person to commit such an act.

Jeremy Joseph Strohmeyer, an adopted child, lived with his father, a military pilot, his mother, and his older sister, Heather, in a variety of locations before the family finally settled in California. As a child Jeremy had attended Christian schools in Cypress; he had been considered an intelligent, out-going boy from his earliest years. For the past several years Strohmeyer and his family had lived in an upscale neighbor-hood in East Long Beach, California, near an impressive golf course and country club. Throughout his elementary school tenure and into his high school years Strohmeyer had had a reputation as a good student with a pleasant personality.

After his graduation from elementary school, Strohmeyer attended high school at Los Alamitos in southern California until 1995, when his parents moved to Singapore, where he attended the American School until June of that year. Follow-ing that, Jeremy went back to California and began attending Woodrow Wilson High School in Long Beach. Throughout his high school years Strohmeyer maintained excellent grades and was a regular honor student. He exhibited an obvious affinity for the sciences, chemistry in particular. In addition to his scholastic achievements, the teenager developed an avid interest in volleyball. According to his high school coach, who had developed a friendship with Strohmeyer over two years, he was bright, sophisticated, and hard working.

By the age of eighteen Strohmeyer was a successful high school senior, and he dreamed of becoming a pilot like his father. He was doing well scholastically and, like most teen-agers, had a best friend, David Cash, whom he had known since the previous year. His most recent school photograph showed a decidedly handsome adolescent with longish, sandy hair and a pleasant expression. However, during the final few months of his senior year, Strohmeyer seemed to change, and not for the better.

During the latter part of his final year in school, Stroh-meyer's life suddenly seemed to disintegrate around him. According to several of his classmates, the teenager had occa-sionally been seen using speed and drinking alcohol. To com-pound matters, his parents had temporarily ordered him out of their house, forcing him to live with friends. One of the

teenager's temporary residences was the guestroom of a girlfriend, who later told reporters that Strohmeyer had become
physically violent with her on at least one occasion: "Once
in the car, he just started beating me up. He was just partying
too much."[14] However, despite the physical assault, Strohmeyer's friend never reported the incident to authorities, and
no charges were filed against him.

Despite the difficulties Strohmeyer faced during those few
months, the teenager was not in obvious difficulty at school or
with the law, and he maintained his close friendship with
David Cash. One official at Woodrow Wilson High School described the teenager during this time as average, not apparently troubled in any significant way: "He does not have an
extensive discipline record. He does not stand out."[15]

For over a year Strohmeyer and Cash had been inseparable,
so it was not unusual when David Cash's father invited his
son's best friend to accompany the pair on a driving trip to Las
Vegas over the long Memorial Day weekend in 1997. The trio
planned to drive along Interstate 15 from southern California,
make their way to Las Vegas, and return in time for the teenagers to be back at school. To break up the long drive, it was
decided that they would stop along the California-Nevada
border to rest, while David's father gambled.

The Primadonna Hotel and Casino is located in Primm,
Nevada, very near the state line, and is an unavoidable land-
mark in the area. This small border town, located directly on
the interstate, survives on the operation of three casinos, which
beckon travelers with a stunning glare of neon in this otherwise dreary and flat part of the southwest. All three casinos are
owned by Primadonna Resorts, Inc., and between them they
offer travelers some three thousand rooms, restaurants, a variety of entertainment, and unlimited gambling. Since the hotels
are adjacent to the only interstate highway between southern
California and Las Vegas, the resorts are often busy on long
weekends and during the peak summer travel months. It was

here at the Primadonna that the Cash party arrived on Sunday, May 25, 1997, on their way to Las Vegas.

The trio planned to only stop for a while to let the teenagers see the sights and get some exercise while David Cash's father gambled in the casino. Since it was a long weekend and the hotel was filled to capacity, the Primadonna arcade was not closed at midnight (as it was usually), and it became the focus of Strohmeyer's and Cash's attention.

On that same weekend Leroy Iverson also arrived at the Primadonna Hotel, shortly after midnight, on a family vacation. He had driven to the resort from his home in south-central Los Angeles, accompanied by his seven-year-old daughter, Sherrice, and her fourteen-year-old brother. However, after arriving at the hotel Iverson discovered that there were no rooms available for the family; he decided to spend the night gambling in the hotel casino, leaving his children on their own.

The second-grader and her older brother walked to another casino across the highway from the Primadonna to look at the sights. Later they returned to the Primadonna, where their father was gambling, and discovered the arcade. While Leroy Iverson continued to gamble, Sherrice and her brother idled away the time separately playing games in the arcade. Two or three times during the early morning hours, security guards discovered the little girl alone and each time called her father from the casino to deal with the situation.

Approximately an hour before Sherrice was seen for the last time, security personnel found her asleep on a chair inside the arcade, once again unattended. According to a hotel spokesperson, each time Leroy Iverson had been contacted by security officers, he had been asked to take his children and leave the casino. However, he never left the Primadonna; Sherrice continued to stay in and around the arcade area, where she eventually met Jeremy Strohmeyer and David Cash.

Shortly after they met, Strohmeyer became involved in a game of hide-and-seek with the little girl. While David Cash continued to be absorbed in video games, Strohmeyer cavorted around the area with Sherrice, playing a variety of games, including a continuing exchange of spitballs and apparently friendly taunts. Unknown to Strohmeyer, the Primadonna Hotel maintained an extensive security system that included video-tape monitors located at strategic points throughout the building. According to the Primadonna videotapes, Strohmeyer followed Sherrice into the women's restroom at 3:48 in the morning, apparently still engaged in hide-and-seek. The time counter on the tape showed that Strohmeyer remained there for about twenty-five minutes. During his stay in the bathroom, which was not covered by a security camera, the tape showed several women entering and exiting the facility, none of whom apparently noticed anything suspicious. However, Sherrice Iverson never left the restroom alive.

What transpired between Sherrice and Strohmeyer was partially witnessed by Strohmeyer's friend, David Cash, who also entered the restroom shortly after the pair but remained there only a few moments. The rest of the gruesome details became known when an affidavit of statements made by Jeremy Strohmeyer to police officers was filed in the Good-springs Justice Court, Nevada, a few weeks later.

When Strohmeyer followed the girl into the restroom, she apparently tossed a "wet floor" sign in his direction, striking him. According to the teenager's later statements to police, this act angered him. Strohmeyer grabbed Sherrice and forced her into the handicapped stall of the restroom, where he put his hand over her mouth because she was struggling to escape. He then lifted the girl onto the top of the toilet and began removing her boots, pants, and underpants; he tossed them into the toilet and sexually assaulted Sherrice with his fingers. During the assault, three women entered the restroom. Fearing that he would be discovered, Strohmeyer sat on top of the little girl and "put her dangling feet in the toilet water so it would look like someone was using the toilet."[16]

After the women left the restroom, Strohmeyer noticed

that Sherrice's breathing was heavy and labored. According to the affidavit, he thought the little girl was brain dead and he did not want her to suffer any longer, so he attempted to break her neck. After his first try, Strohmeyer realized that Sherrice was still alive, so he repeated the attempt. This time, Strohmeyer determined that his victim was no longer breathing, and he quickly exited the restroom, leaving Sherrice Iverson's body in the stall.

Approximately forty-five minutes after Strohmeyer left the restroom, Leroy Iverson asked hotel security personnel to help find his daughter, who he thought should have still been in or around the arcade area with her brother. At approximately 5:30 in the morning a hotel security officer found Sherrice's body, still sitting on the toilet in the closed stall of the women's restroom. She had been dead for over an hour, and it was quickly determined that she had been sexually molested and strangled.

Meanwhile, David Cash, his father, and Jeremy Strohmeyer had left the Primadonna for their final destination. They arrived in Las Vegas on Sunday night and checked into a downtown motel. The following morning the trio returned to Southern California, the details of the murder of Sherrice Iverson known only to the two teenagers.

According to the hotel videotape, about ten minutes after leaving the restroom, Strohmeyer and Cash left the hotel together through the swimming pool entrance. Based on David Cash's later testimony before a grand jury, it was at this point that Strohmeyer told his friend that he had murdered the seven-year-old. According to Cash, the subject of Sherrice Iverson's murder was not discussed throughout the remainder of the holiday weekend.

After the trio returned to California, Strohmeyer began discussing the murder of Iverson with some of his friends. It was not long before the combination of news reports of Sherrice's murder, television broadcasts of the Primadonna videotapes, and gossip about Strohmeyer's bragging came to the attention of David Cash's father and Strohmeyer's girlfriend's parents. Horrified by what they heard, the parents immediately notified police of their suspicions.

On Wednesday night, May 28, 1997, Jeremy Strohmeyer was arrested at his parents' home in Long Beach, just two weeks before he would have graduated from high school. Throughout the evening officers had kept the Strohmeyer home under surveillance; he was apprehended without incident as he left the residence through a side door.

Immediately after he was arrested, the teenager told investigating officers that he had just ingested an undetermined quantity of prescription medications. Police quickly transported Strohmeyer to a local hospital, where he was treated and released without any significant complications. One of the officers involved in the arrest called the teenager's drug ingestion "a halfhearted suicide attempt."[17] However, it was not clear whether the teenager had actually attempted to kill himself or was merely high on drugs.

Shortly after Strohmeyer was taken into custody he made several statements to authorities that implicated him in the murder of Sherrice Iverson. According to investigators, the teenager's conversation was damning enough to be considered a confession to the crime. However, these statements were later sealed by the court at the request of Strohmeyer's defense attorney, who questioned whether they had been obtained legally. In addition to the teenager's statements, however, in

---

Snapshot Profile of Jeremy Strohmeyer

An eighteen-year-old high school honor student whose life had begun to collapse shortly before graduation. Without purpose or warning, Strohmeyer brutally molested and murdered a seven-year-old girl in the women's restroom of a Nevada casino while on a trip with his best friend.

vestigators had already collected considerable forensic evidence that linked him to the crime. To further solidify the case against him, Strohmeyer's friend, David Cash, had voluntarily surrendered to authorities to offer what he knew of the crime, which was sufficient to convince investigators that Strohmeyer had acted alone in murdering the little girl.

Based on what police learned on May 28 and 29, Strohmeyer was ordered to be held without bail at the Long Beach City Jail to await an extradition hearing for his eventual return to Nevada. He was also placed on a suicide watch; attending officers remained uncertain about his intentions in taking drugs shortly before his arrest, and about his emotional state.

In a bizarre and disturbing twist to the horrible fate of Sherrice Iverson, the actions of her father after her death also came to be of interest to investigators. According to hotel personnel, Leroy Iverson had asked for compensation shortly after he learned of his daughter's murder. Chris Gibase, the chief operating officer for the Primadonna Hotel and Casino, described Iverson's reaction to his daughter's murder this way: "He [Iverson] said he wouldn't sue anybody if they would give him $100 to gamble with, free beer, fly his girlfriend in from out of town, and he wanted money for the arcade for the fourteen-year-old boy. His cavalier attitude was so shocking, everyone was stunned."[18] Iverson later denied making these comments to hotel officials, claiming that he had asked nothing of the Primadonna. However, he did engage an attorney to represent his position in any future encounters with the press.

For the next few months, the details of the death of Sherrice Iverson, and what little was known of Jeremy Strohmeyer, captured headlines across the nation. However, despite intense press investigation into the case, the teenager charged with such a brutal crime remained a confusing figure to those who did not know him well.

On August 1, 1997, after his extradition to Nevada, Jeremy Strohmeyer was formally indicted on charges of murder, first-degree kidnapping, and two counts of sexual assault against a minor. Because it had been decided by Las Vegas officials that he would be tried as an adult, the teenager was faced with the possibility of the death penalty if found guilty of the charges against him. In late August 1997, Strohmeyer formally pleaded innocent to all counts.

On the day of his appearance in court, it was obvious to reporters that the adolescent had undergone a startling physical transformation during his months of imprisonment. His once blonde, long hair had been darkened, severely cropped, and spiked, and he had lost a substantial amount of weight. Reports in the press indicated that he had received repeated death threats from other inmates because of the brutal nature of the crime and the extensive news coverage of his case, particularly in the Las Vegas area. However, the teenager still remained an enigmatic figure to court observers, the media, and the public. On September 8, 1998, Strohmeyer plead guilty to charges of murder, kidnapping, and sexual assault. At the age of 19, he was sentenced to life in prison without the possibility of parole.

Speaking to the press about her client and the charges against him, famed defense attorney Leslie Abramson, who had once represented the Menendez brothers in their murder trial, summed up what many felt about Jeremy Strohmeyer: "There are a lot of mysteries in this case, not the least of which is the mystery of my client."[19]

SENSELESS CULT MURDERS

The history of cult activities in America is a long and sometimes sordid one. Since the 1960s we have become more cognizant of cult activities and, as parents, more concerned about the growing number of our children who have joined a wide variety of strange and sometimes aggressive cults. Much of this renewed awareness of cult activities stems from the highly publicized accounts of violent or illegal activities ascribed to a few radical and aggressive groups. However, cults can also be highly organized, well funded, and large in terms of their membership and impact on our society.

Certainly, few Americans are unaware of the tragedy of Jonestown in 1978, in which more than nine hundred members of a religious cult took their own lives at the direction of the organization's founder, Jim Jones. This horrible incident claimed massive headlines in the press and even riveted the attention of legislators at the federal level. In fact, the Jonestown tragedy opened a new era in our awareness and fear of cults. Prior to Jonestown, cults had been generally recognized as aberrations in our societal structure or at most, groups of easily led, nonviolent individuals who were obviously being manipulated by their leaders. However, the mass suicide at Jonestown changed our basic assumption about the power and potential danger of cult activities in this country.

In 1993, fifteen years after the Jonestown suicides, David Koresh led his cult, the Branch Davidians, into an armed confrontation with the FBI and the Bureau of Alcohol, Tobacco, and Firearms in Waco, Texas. The result of this confrontation was the death of nearly a hundred cult members when their compound burned to the ground with its occupants trapped inside. Sadly, many of the victims were children. The Branch Davidians had been convinced by their leader that the end of the world was at hand. When federal law enforcement officers surrounded the cult's compound in an attempt to arrest their leader, Koresh, they gave apparent substance to his claims of the impending end of civilization. Through a series of blunders, miscommunications, and poor decisions, the culmination of the standoff at Waco was the death of nearly all the Branch Davidians, including Koresh.

As evidenced by such notorious cases as Jonestown and the Branch Davidians, cults are not uniform in their size, structure, or beliefs. In fact, these organizations are extremely varied in their scope, intent, and purpose. They can range from large, international, multigeneration groups, to local and independent associations, to ill-defined groups of two or three persons, and even a single individual who has involved himself or herself in activities loosely affiliated with a larger, more recognized cult. However, when a cult of several or more individuals is formed, the association takes on a profile that is consistent, identifiable, and sometimes dangerous.

Regardless of their size or complexity, these groups invariably come together around an individual who has a strong, dominant personality and an ability to organize others in a powerful, manipulative way. Such charismatic leaders, who often employ strong religious or anti-religious themes in their teachings, form the root of the cult, define its purpose, and dictate the activities of cult members to an extent that is sometimes phenomenal. In essence, the leader of a cult is typically viewed as omnipotent and all-powerful by his or her followers, while the members of the organization are relegated to a subservient, highly dependent role.

In recent decades there has been a troubling increase in the number of teenagers who have joined established cults or who have come together in small groups to form their own, loose associations based on identifiable cult activities. Much of this interest in cults seems to center around an adolescent's feelings of separateness from the adult world around him and the need for a special closeness and unity with his peers. Beyond this, the charismatic and dynamic personality of the cult leader offers a strong lure to teenagers, who can easily feel displaced, abandoned, and unrecognized in their more traditional social circles.

Teenage cult activities frequently involve drug use and can sometimes result in violent or suicidal behavior. This is particularly true when the association involves a belief system that vehemently disdains traditional societal norms or devalues the sacredness of life, as may be the case with some extremist satanic cults. Fortunately, such extremism is relatively rare among teenage cult members. However, when these groups do become violent, their crimes are often exceptionally brutal and senseless. Shockingly, it is not uncommon for murderous cult members to be identified later as individuals without any previous history of violence or conflict with the law. However, in other cases, homicidal cult members were aggressive, violent individuals who only actuated their full murderous potential within the activities of the organization they led.

For example, in the early 1980s Robin Gecht formed a loose association of four satanic cultists around his own, bizarre concepts of good and evil. Gecht was a former employee of the notorious serial killer John Wayne Gacy, and an individual who knew no limits to his own outrageous behavior. Together with three friends, Gecht organized a satanic cult that specialized in the murder of prostitutes in the Chicago area. These violent cultists viewed their horrible acts of mutilation and murder as "sacrifices" made in the name of Satan. By the time they were arrested in 1982, the cult members had brutally slain at least eight women. In each case, not only was the victim mutilated, but the perpetrators had ritually eaten parts of her body.

Ten years later, in 1993, another loosely formed cult murdered three eight-year-old boys in what proved to be an impromptu, vicious attempt to perform a satanic ritual. Damien Wayne Echols, a nineteen-year-old self-styled satanist, organized a cult that consisted of two of his friends, Jason Baldwin and Jesse Lloyd Misskelley. All three were involved in drug abuse and minor criminal activities, and Baldwin and Misskelley easily fell under the control of the dominant Echols. On May 5, 1993, the three eight-year-olds were riding their bicycles in the Robin Hood Hills area in West Memphis when Echols and his cohorts attacked them. The three children were tied, stripped of their clothing, severely beaten, and murdered. One of the boys was sexually mutilated in an exceptionally brutal way.

Although this gruesome crime took some time to solve, the three perpetrators were eventually brought to justice and were tried for their crimes in 1994. Misskelley was tried first, found guilty, and sentenced to life in prison plus forty years. A month after Misskelley was sentenced, the cult leader, Echols, and his friend, Baldwin, were tried and found guilty of murder. Baldwin was sentenced to life in prison without the possibility of parole, and Echols was sentenced to die by lethal injection.

From time to time, an individual teenager becomes deeply involved with cult-like beliefs and activities that lead to violence and death without the participation of another individual. In such cases the adolescent takes on the philosophy and behavior of other cultists with whom he has become familiar through literature or personal exposure. Although relatively rare, these individuals sometimes commit murder and point to their bizarre and violent philosophical beliefs as the primary motivation for their crimes. As in the case of more organized cults with adolescent members, these isolated teenagers are often involved in drug use.

At the age of seventeen, Nathan Brooks became heavily involved in satanism, the occult in general, and rituals of black magic in particular. On September 30, 1995, the teenager murdered his mother with an ax, shot his father, and then decapitated him with a hacksaw in their family home in Ohio. Brooks was promptly arrested, confessed to the murders, and explained to investigators that he planned to use his father's severed head in a black magic ritual. When police investigated Brooks's room they found overwhelming evidence of his obsession with satanism and black magic, including paraphernalia to be used in the planned ritual with his father's head. When he was tried for murder, Brooks unsuccessfully claimed that he had been insane at the time of the crime.

In California, in the summer of 1995, three teenagers drugged a fifteen-year-old girl, abducted her, and took her to a secluded area near her home. In a thick grove of trees the teenagers beat the girl, raped her, cinched a belt around her neck to control her, and stabbed her to death on an impromptu altar the attackers had arranged. The perpetrators were fifteen, sixteen, and seventeen years old—all members of a cult dedicated to satanism. The victim was originally reported as a missing person, and investigators were unable to generate significant leads in the case for nearly two years. However, in early 1996 one of the members of the cult confessed to his participation in the murder and led investigators to the victim's body.

A year after this grisly homicide in California, four teenagers and an adult in Kentucky were arrested for murdering a Florida couple in a cult attack apparently related to the practice of vampirism. The victims were the parents of one of the members of a self-styled cult that practiced a mishmash of bizarre rituals, including the sacrifice of small animals and drinking of blood. Each of the members of the cult took on special nicknames—a practice reminiscent of the followers of Charles Manson—and each played his or her part as a vampire by wearing ritualistic dress and meeting with other cult members for a variety of secret and strange practices. The leader of this cult, who referred to herself as "Heather," claimed to be the reincarnation of a demon who had the ability to speak with other demons during her blood-drinking rituals. Over time, the vampire cult members developed increasingly odd and violent behavior, culminating in the bludgeoning death of one of the member's parents.

Obviously, not all aggressive and illegal cult activities result in a violent attack on others. In fact, some of this behavior can devolve into a moment of self-destructive behavior that is equally tragic and senseless. In 1996, two high school students entered into a satanic pact to commit suicide and then carried out their own executions. Both boys were sixteen years old and described as well-adjusted teenagers, good students, and nonviolent individuals without any criminal history. In fact, one of the teenagers was an honor student, and the other had maintained an excellent academic record. However, both became deeply interested in satanic rituals and black magic shortly before their deaths. Those who knew the adolescents later told investigators that their involvement in satanism and black magic was much more than a passing fancy—it had become an obvious obsession for these best friends.

On September 20, 1996, both teenagers were reported missing by their parents, along with a 9-mm automatic and a .38-caliber handgun. The teenagers had arranged their own deaths, stolen the handguns, and met at a landfill area near their homes. There, each committed suicide with the handgun he had brought along. When investigators examined the boys' residences, they found in excess of a hundred pieces of evidence linking the teenagers to a variety of satanic ritualistic practices, including a tape recorded suicide message from the boys, which indicated the bizarre philosophical motivation for the double suicide.

Much has been made in the media about the violence that is so often associated with cults. In fact, some estimates of the annual number of homicides attributed to cult activities exceeds the number of known murders in this country by more than double. Clearly, there is a great deal of concern about the involvement of our teenagers in cult activities, and there also appears to be a good deal of sensationalism surrounding the subject. However, the potential impact of these activities on our children should not be minimized. Certainly, the gruesome crimes of Charles Manson and his followers three decades ago is a stark lesson in how our children can be led and manipulated by a dominant, tragically misdirected individual.

As parents, it is particularly important that we understand as much as possible about the activities of our children, without unduly interfering in their lives. This is particularly important if a teenager begins to drift into a nefarious world of secret rituals or falls under the influence of a single, dominant individual. Sudden, unexplained changes in behavior, extreme secretiveness, the unexpected appearance of repeated criminal behavior, animal mutilation, unusual or bizarre dress or body markings, or the expression of intense hatred for ethnic, religious or minority groups can be indicators that a teenager has become affiliated with a cult or has succumbed to the influence of a powerful personality. Clearly, such changes in a teenager are warnings of undesirable and potentially violent behavior patterns that should not be ignored. At this crucial time—when an adolescent is about to become deeply involved in cult activities—he or she is in an extremely tenuous and dangerous position. It is at this moment that the teenager needs the complete involvement and love of his or her parents, possibly in conjunction with professional help, to avoid a potentially disastrous and life-altering outcome.

A MURDER OF OBSESSION

Violent crimes that are prompted by a sexual or romantic obsession are not infrequent in this country. When such an obsession results in murder, the crime can be exceptionally brutal and may sometimes claim more lives than the unfortunate target of the murderer's obsession. For law enforcement personnel, homicides of this type have an obvious and troubling pattern, which is usually apparent from the behavior of the perpetrator and forensic evidence collected at the crime scene. However, these crimes are not often associated with young teenagers, which makes the case of Edward O'Brien, Jr., both disturbing and unique.

O'Brien was a former altar boy with no history of violence and no criminal record, who lived in a quiet area of Somerville, Massachusetts. Like most teenagers, he had a best friend, Ryan Downing, who lived across the street and with whom he spent a good deal of time. To his neighbors and friends, O'Brien, the son of the former police chief of Somerville, seemed to be an ordinary and innocuous teenager, except for one peculiar trait—he had an abiding and obvious interest in his best friend's mother, Janet Downing.

By 1995, at the age of fifteen, Edward O'Brien had developed into an imposing teenager; he stood well over six feet tall and weighed 260 pounds. By this time, it was well known to

Ryan Downing that his best friend delighted in spying on Janet Downing from across the street, usually trying to get glimpses of her while she was undressing in the evening. Also, because of his close friendship with Ryan, O'Brien was a frequent visitor at the Downing residence, where his interest in Mrs. Downing had become apparent to family members. However, O'Brien was invariably polite and unassertive with Ryan's mother and her sons, as he was with all who knew him.

On the evening of July 23, 1995, Janet Downing was brutally murdered in her home, attacked when napping on the living room couch. The assault on Downing had been an extraordinarily vicious one; she was stabbed ninety-eight times. Virtually every part of the victim's body had been slashed, except for her breasts. Downing's neck area alone had received at least twenty stab wounds, any of several of which were fatal.

It was the victim's seventeen-year-old son Ryan who found his mother's body when he returned home that evening after spending time with friends. To his horror, Ryan found his mother lying unconscious in a pool of blood and immediately ran across the street to his best friend's house for help. However, Edward O'Brien was not at home; rather, O'Brien's father answered the door. He immediately called for medical aid for Janet Downing, while he tried to comfort Ryan.

When paramedics arrived at the Downing house a few moments later, she had already suffered such a massive loss of blood that she could not be saved. Attending medical and forensic personnel noted the nearly hundred stab wounds and a variety of bruises and scrapes, and that she had apparently been undressed and dressed again sometime during the attack. There was no evidence of rape at the crime scene; however, it was obvious that the victim had struggled furiously for her life during an attack that was probably sexually motivated.

Law enforcement officers arrived at the Downing home shortly after paramedics to begin their investigation. It was during those first chaotic moments, when Edward O'Brien, Sr., was still with Ryan Downing, that the elder O'Brien learned why his son was not at home. According to information from arriving police officers, O'Brien, Jr., had been mugged and robbed at approximately the same time Janet Downing had been attacked.

According to the younger O'Brien's statements to police, two unidentified men had assaulted and robbed him at knife-point behind the Somerville police department. However, despite obvious injuries, O'Brien had not immediately sought help at the nearby police department. Instead, he had walked a few blocks to a local convenience store, where he held a part-time job assembling newspapers for sale. Witnesses at the convenience store later told police that O'Brien had arrived at about ten o'clock that evening looking sweaty, pale, and with blood and scrapes on his legs. He was also bleeding from the palm of one of his hands.

In fact, O'Brien's appearance caused enough concern that one of the store employees insistently questioned him about what had happened and demanded that he receive medical assistance. The teenager told his coworker that he had just been mugged behind the police station and, as if to convince the employee of the events he was describing, held up his right hand to clearly show wounds that appeared to have been made by a knife. Based on the story O'Brien told his coworkers, a convenience store employee called the police. That call was placed less than ten minutes after the Somerville police had been notified about the attack on Janet Downing.

When interviewed later that evening, O'Brien told law enforcement officers that two African-American males had attacked him and stolen eighteen dollars in cash. The unidentified attackers, he said, had also tried to stab him, but he had grabbed the knife blade in an effort to defend himself, thereby receiving the gashes on the palm of his hand. However, there were inconsistencies in O'Brien's story that troubled investigators from the beginning. Later that night, when police examined the scene of the alleged mugging to find substantiation for O'Brien's claim, no supporting evidence could be located.

Investigators were intensely suspicious of O'Brien's move-
ments on the night of July 23, 1995, and soon came to suspect
him of murder when they learned that he had been seen at the
back of Janet Downing's home shortly before Ryan returned
home to find his dying mother. Friends of Ryan's reported to
police that they had seen O'Brien at the scene of the crime
around 9:30 that evening, acting in a strange manner, apparently hiding in some bushes on the Downing property. They
also noticed that the cellar door of the Downing home had
been thrown open. When one of the teenagers approached
O'Brien and commented about his hiding in the bushes, he
had hurriedly left the area without speaking.

Given this witness information, the background profile
they had developed about the teenager, the statements of the
convenience store employees, and a preliminary crime scene
analysis, police were convinced that O'Brien had been Janet
Downing's attacker. On July 26, 1995, they arrested the teenager and charged him with first-degree murder.

For the next two years, O'Brien awaited his fate while
prosecutors worked feverishly to ensure that he would be tried
as an adult. The exceptionally vicious murder of Janet Downing outraged both legislators and the public, and created sensational headlines in the local press. In fact, it was the case
against O'Brien that prompted the state of Massachusetts to
pass a new law requiring that any teenager over the age of
fourteen who was charged with a capital crime be tried as an
adult. Given the unprecedented public pressure to deal harshly
with the murderer of Janet Downing, prosecutors involved
with O'Brien's case were eventually successful in their demands that the teenager not be tried as a juvenile.

On September 18, 1997, Edward O'Brien's trial for first-
degree murder began. The case for the prosecution was based
on the theory that O'Brien had become hopelessly obsessed
with Janet Downing and that this obsession had finally driven
him to murder her in a sexual rage. During the course of the
trial, prosecutors called a number of witnesses to substantiate

their claim of obsession and demonstrate that the murder had been premeditated. Among these witnesses was O'Brien's coworker at the convenience store, who testified that the teenager had shown him a unique knife with a green handle prior to July 23, 1995. Investigators at the crime scene had discovered part of a knife with a similar green handle on the evening of Janet Downing's murder. However, they never found the complete murder weapon in the case, nor were they able to specifically link the part of the knife found at the crime scene to Edward O'Brien.

As with the issue of the murder weapon, the remainder of the case against Edward O'Brien was largely circumstantial; however, it was quite powerful. Prosecutors produced testimony from investigating officers that the murder of Janet Downing met the classic profile of a crime of rage and sexual obsession. Criminologists noted that a number of blood smears had been discovered in the Downing home, made by the attacker after the victim had succumbed to her wounds. Some of these smears had been discovered on clothes hung in the backyard of Downing's house, where O'Brien had been seen on the night of the murder by witnesses. A fingerprint expert testified that O'Brien's bloody fingerprints had been discovered inside the front door of the Downing home and in a second location in the cellar. Finally, other forensic evidence,

---

Snapshot Profile of Edward O'Brien, Jr.

A fifteen-year-old former altar boy who had no history of violence or criminal activities. However, the teenager was obviously obsessed with the mother of his best friend, who lived across the street from O'Brien. In a rage, he brutally murdered Janet Downing by stabbing her ninety-eight times in a crime that was sexually motivated. O'Brien stood trial as an adult, was found guilty of first-degree murder, and was sentenced to life in prison without the possibility of parole.

such as blood of the victim's type discovered on O'Brien's pants and the presence of the teenager's DNA in the Downing home, demonstrated his presence at the crime scene.

The combined testimony of prosecution witnesses and crime scene evidence was strong, and it indicated that O'Brien had probably laid in wait for Janet Downing on the evening of July 23, 1995, to be sure she was alone. When he was convinced that he would be unseen and uninterrupted, the teenager had entered the home through the cellar door and moved upstairs to where the victim was sleeping on her living room couch. There, he brutally attacked Janet Downing, undressed her, dressed her again, and made his way from the crime scene to his part-time job at the convenience store.

Janet Downing's sons, including Ryan, testified extensively about O'Brien's obvious obsession with their mother, citing a variety of incidents and odd patterns of behavior to support their claim. The defense team countered this argument by eliciting testimony that indicated the teenager was never hostile or aggressive with the victim, even though he admittedly exhibited an unusual interest in her. However, when taken together, the statements in court painted the portrait of a teenager who had become obsessed with his victim and probably murdered her in a rage.

The defense team argued that O'Brien could not have murdered Janet Downing, because he had not been in the vicinity of her home at the time of the crime. According to O'Brien's statements to police, he was being attacked and robbed at about the same time the murder took place. Moreover, O'Brien's attorneys pointed out that their defendant had demonstrated no history of violence or involvement with the law and was therefore a most unlikely suspect in the case. O'Brien's defense team also claimed that investigators had made a number of serious mistakes at the crime scene that resulted in false charges against their client. They argued that conflicting forensic evidence and poor crime-scene control could not rule out the presence of a third, unidentified individual in the Downing home on the night of the murder. Finally, the defense team noted that investigators had focused immediately and solely on their client, disregarding any possibility that another individual had actually murdered Janet Downing.

On September 30, 1997, the jury heard final arguments in the case and began its deliberations. The next day, after a total of ten hours of deliberation, it found Edward O'Brien guilty of first-degree murder. In accordance with Massachusetts law, the teenager was immediately sentenced to life in prison without the possibility of parole.

The murder of Janet Downing was not only senseless and brutal, but it prompted a new and harsher view of teenage violence in Massachusetts. Such tougher legislation is becoming more evident throughout our country as outraged citizens and lawmakers try to establish a level of control over crimes that are, at their root, incomprehensible in their viciousness. However, as in the case of Edward O'Brien, there is a troubling general silence on the issues of prevention and intervention, combined with an apparent sense of helplessness—that little could have been done to prevent such a murder in the first place. Beyond this, there is always the question of motivation, which often remains unanswered to the satisfaction of many.

Certainly, as a society, we cannot continue to succumb to the understandable sense of helplessness and uncertainty that accompanies such an unexpected and brutal crime. Nor can we rely solely on punishment after the fact to hold back the increasing level of violent juvenile crime in this country. We must look much deeper than our judicial or social systems if we are to address this challenge in the future. We must begin to look into the role of the family as our first and best line of prevention and defense; as several case histories in this book have already demonstrated, it is often the family that is the target of adolescent violence.

Senseless Family Murders

The murders committed in 1993 by Andrew DeYoung rank among the most grizzly and difficult to explain among the many cases of apparently good kids who have gone horribly wrong. Like so many other adolescents who commit extraordinarily brutal acts of violence, DeYoung had no criminal record and no history of violence before he murdered three members of his family. In fact, he was a highly intelligent honor student who had been raised in a deeply religious, close-knit family.

Unlike teenagers who attack their family members in a moment of uncontrolled rage, DeYoung planned and carried out his crimes in a precise and methodical manner. However, despite strong indications of premeditation, the physical evidence at the crime scene indicated that the homicides were committed with a level of brutality that was exceptionally vicious and unnecessary to the apparent motivation for the attack—profit. In this sense the murders committed by Andrew DeYoung are enigmatic, and the known facts of the case remain contradictory in many respects.

At the age of nineteen, Andrew Grant DeYoung was a business major at Kennesaw State College in Georgia, a straight-A student and a member of the National Honor Society. His background had been nonviolent and unremarkable, and the teenager was widely recognized as bright and inquisitive. Andrew lived with his parents, younger brother, and younger sister in a comfortable, upper-middle-class, religiously oriented family environment. Throughout his childhood Andrew had been known as a serious and stable individual, devoted to his family.

On June 14, 1993, Gary and Kathy DeYoung, Andrew's parents, had just returned from an anniversary trip. That evening, as was their habit, they attended a local church service with their two other children, Sarah and Nathan. At around three o'clock in the morning, two men dressed in dark, para-military style clothing suddenly invaded the DeYoung home and brutally attacked the family, without any apparent motive. In a matter of moments, three of the four family members lay dead: Gary DeYoung, 41, Kathy DeYoung, also 41, and Sarah DeYoung, age 14. The only survivor was Nathan DeYoung, age 16, who had been able to escape from the family home after hearing the assault against his sister. The teenager briefly tried to telephone for emergency assistance but had found that the line was dead—it had been cut from outside the home. In desperation, Nathan pushed his way through a window in the home and fled to a neighbor's house for help. Unfortunately, in the darkness and chaos Nathan had been unable to get a good look at the intruders.

When the bodies of the victims were found by responding law enforcement officers, the DeYoung home proved to be a horrific crime scene. Gary and Kathy DeYoung were found slumped to the floor, lying near the foot of their bed. They had been stabbed dozens of times, and their throats had been slit. Sarah DeYoung's body was discovered in the upstairs hallway. Like her parents, her throat had been slit. She had been stabbed more than forty times.

The neighbor who had come to the aid of Nathan DeYoung had seen Andrew outside the family home after the attack, and

---

Snapshot Profile of Andrew DeYoung

A nineteen-year-old honor student who had no criminal record or history of violence. With an accomplice, DeYoung carefully planned and carried out the exceptionally brutal execution of three members of his family, allegedly to inherit their wealth. DeYoung was arrested, tried, found guilty on three counts of murder, and sentenced to death. His accomplice avoided the death penalty by testifying against DeYoung at his trial.

he became an immediate suspect in the case. He was arrested the next day on suspicion of murder. He immediately and adamantly proclaimed his innocence; nonetheless, officials had sufficient evidence to hold him and formally charge him with three counts of murder. Also apprehended for murder was David Haggerty, as DeYoung's co-conspirator in the crime.

The murderous attack on the DeYoung family was described in the press as "a precisely planned, commando-style raid staged by Andrew Grant DeYoung."[20] From the beginning of the investigation phase of the case, officials were convinced that DeYoung had murdered his family so that he could receive an insurance settlement and, later, the family estate. Although estimates of the value of the DeYoung estate varied, most believed it to be between $750,000 and $900,000, much of it tied up in the family home. Later court testimony from DeYoung's accomplice in the crime indicated that the teenager wanted to raise capital to finance his plans for either a movie theatre or a youth entertainment business. This became the clear motivation needed to prosecute Andrew DeYoung successfully.

In 1994, David Michael Haggerty confessed to his role in the murders, although he denied anything more incriminating than his presence at the planning of the crime and later at the scene of the killings. Under an arrangement with prosecutors, Haggerty testified against Andrew DeYoung in exchange for the prosecution's agreement not to seek the death penalty in his case. In November of that year Haggerty entered a formal guilty plea to three counts of murder and was sentenced to three life terms in prison.

David Haggerty claimed that DeYoung had often discussed killing his family and that DeYoung had aggressively recruited him into the crime plan, which involved not only murder but the destruction of the DeYoung family home by arson to cover up the crime. According to his accomplice, DeYoung had been very methodical in his planning, even organizing a precise scheme to approach the house unheard and unseen, complete with a detailed map of the route to the home and the home itself. The murder plan included the use of dark paramilitary clothing to disguise the identity of the attackers. It was this garb that led to Nathan DeYoung's inability to identify any of the intruders on June 14, 1993.

However, there were troubling inconsistencies in the case from the beginning. For example, neither Haggerty nor anyone else could explain the apparent contradiction between DeYoung's plan to murder for profit and his intention to destroy the assets that he hoped to inherit. In any case, according to Haggerty's explanation, the pair panicked and fled from the DeYoung home without setting it ablaze when a neighbor armed with a handgun appeared on the scene. In addition, the nature of the murders was troubling. Even a cursory review of forensic and medical evidence in the case clearly indicated the exceptional brutality of the attack. Each of the victims had been stabbed repeatedly and with obvious rage and viciousness. Clearly, for a murder for profit, the gruesome nature of the attack indicated an emotional state of mind that was anything but cool and cold-blooded, as Andrew DeYoung had been consistently portrayed in the media.

When the attack on the DeYoung family took place, Haggerty claimed he had been unable to go through with his end of the arrangement, which was to murder Andrew DeYoung's younger brother, Nathan. He went on to say that Andrew had taken him into his parents' bedroom and showed Haggerty the result of his gruesome handiwork. Throughout his statements to police and prosecutors, as well as his later court testimony, Haggerty persistently minimized his role in the crime and consistently pointed to Andrew DeYoung as the mastermind of the attack and sole executioner of the victims. However, the question of motive remained a point of controversy for some.

When Nathan DeYoung was asked in court why, in his opinion, Andrew murdered his family, the teenager seemed uncertain. He confirmed that he had never heard Andrew threaten his family and had not known him to ever be aggressive or violent in the family home. However, Nathan did point out that Andrew had resented having to attend church with the family as a condition of living at home and that his older brother had sometimes spoken of plans for the future that required money.

Throughout the trial, Andrew DeYoung's defense team argued that the case against their client was in effect a conspiratorial arrangement between prosecuting attorneys and DeYoung's accomplice, David Haggerty. Since Haggerty had avoided the possibility of the death penalty by agreeing to testify against DeYoung, the defense team claimed that his version of events was tainted, self-serving, and untrue. Beyond this, they argued that it was Haggerty himself, along with an unknown third person, who had actually committed the murders. Since David Haggerty was already a convicted burglar who had now confessed to participating in murder, DeYoung's defense attorneys hoped to destroy Haggerty's credibility as a witness and throw doubt into the jury's mind about their client's involvement in the crime.

However, the jury was not persuaded by the defense position. In October 1995, Andrew DeYoung was found guilty of three counts of murder. During the penalty phase of his trial, an emotional plea was made by DeYoung's grandparents to spare him from death and sentence him to life in prison without the possibility of parole. However, because of the heinous nature of the murders and the compelling evidence of careful planning, the jury recommended a sentence of death.

In many ways, the crimes for which Andrew DeYoung may die are exceptionally troubling. If he was, in fact, a ruthless, cold-blooded killer who carefully planned and carried out the execution of his family, then there is difficulty explaining the rage-like nature of the attack itself. Whoever murdered three members of the DeYoung family did so with a level of passion and brutality that implies a deep, pathological element inherent in their actions. That Andrew DeYoung was highly intelligent and aloof seems relatively certain; however, we do not know anything of his deep, and perhaps dark, feelings about his family. There can be little question that the teenager was capable of planning such an attack, at least from the stand-point of his obvious intelligence. However, there are elements in the crime itself that seem to belie the convicted murderer's alleged intent. Once again, the question of true motivation looms large.

In many ways, this gruesome attack has close parallels with murders committed by adolescents in an uncontrolled, lethal rage—or at least a crime scene that looked that way. Was an abiding, lethal rage at the heart of the DeYoung family murders, or was the crime motive as straightforward as prose-cutors claimed it to be? It is doubtful that we will ever know.

Premeditated but Unexplained

Like Andrew DeYoung, Gweneviere Gardner was an honor student and, until 1994, a nonviolent, stable child. She had no criminal history, nor did she exhibit any indication of signifi-cant behavioral problems. However, Gardner, known to her friends and family as "Wendy," had faced many difficulties in her young life. She was the daughter of a prostitute and drug abuser, who had died after contracting AIDS. Wendy's father, also a drug abuser, had been responsible for the death of her grandfather during a violent physical argument. At the age of five, Wendy and her sister, then three years old, had been taken to live with her grandmother, Betty Gardner.

Despite her troubled family background, by the age of thir-teen Wendy seemed to have completely overcome the difficul-ties of her past. As she entered her teens she had developed into a pretty, soft-spoken individual, who earned excellent grades in school, played the flute, and was considered to be polite and happy by friends and neighbors. Her grandmother, Betty, was sixty-seven years old and deeply religious. She was also a strict disciplinarian, who could be sometimes harsh with Wendy and her younger sister, Kathy.

In October 1994, Wendy, now thirteen, met James Evans, a fifteen-year-old who had a history of stealing bicycles and torturing cats. Shortly after meeting Evans, Wendy underwent a startling personality change. She began to miss days at school, her grades dropped significantly, and she spent more and more time with Evans at his family home. Despite the obvious deterioration in Wendy's previously stable behavior, she claimed to be deeply in love with Evans and wanted nothing more from life but to spend her time with him.

In December 1994, Wendy spent most of two weeks with Evans and his mother in their home. By this time, Betty Gardner was beside herself with Wendy's unacceptable behavior and demanded that her granddaughter immediately return home. On the evening of December 29, 1994, Wendy came back to her grandmother's house, accompanied by James Evans. Shortly after the pair arrived Betty Gardner told Evans to leave her home, and an argument ensued. During the encounter, Evans lunged at Gardner and grabbed her around the neck in a chokehold. Still holding the struggling woman by one arm, he pulled a length of kite string from his pocket and wrapped it around Gardner's neck. In a few moments the woman was dead from strangulation.

While Evans was strangling Betty Gardner, Wendy was in another room of the house with her younger sister, allegedly trying to ignore the gruesome sounds of her grandmother's death struggle. However, when Evans had completed his attack, Wendy helped the murderer hide the victim's body in the trunk of her grandmother's car. In order to keep the crime secret, Wendy physically threatened her younger sister and forcibly kept her under constant surveillance for the next three days. Wendy and James spent that time having sex, playing video games, and shopping with 880 dollars they had stolen from Betty Gardner's purse.

On the third day after the murder, Kathy Gardner was able to escape from her grandmother's home and make her way to a neighbor's house for help. Hearing the frightened girl's story of murder, the neighbor immediately contacted police. Responding officers quickly discovered Betty Gardner's body and arrested Wendy Gardner and James Evans on suspicion of murder. Investigating officers soon came to the conclusion that Wendy and James had planned the murder of Betty Gardner for weeks in advance. They also believed that Wendy had masterminded the crime and convinced Evans to participate. Evans's statements to police supported this version of the crime.

In July 1995, James Evans went to trial. His defense was based on the argument that he had been so controlled by his thirteen-year-old girlfriend that he committed murder for her. However, his defense proved implausible. Evans was convicted of second-degree murder and sentenced to the maximum penalty for his crime—nine years to life in prison.

In February 1997, Wendy Gardner went to trial on the charge of murder—as an adult. During the trial prosecutors portrayed a young teenager who had willfully plotted the murder of her grandmother and then recruited her lover to accomplish the deed. They argued that premeditation was clearly in evidence and that the girl had shown a lack of remorse, by her behavior during the three days after the crime had been committed. Wendy's defense team argued that it was their client who had fallen under the spell of James Evans, an older

---

Snapshot Profile of Wendy Gardner

A thirteen-year-old who had apparently overcome a troubling childhood background and was developing into a promising adolescent. Wendy had no criminal record or history of violence. Shortly after meeting an older teenager, James Evans, she plotted the death of her grandmother for reasons she has never been able to explain. Both Gardner and Evans were arrested, brought to trial, and found guilty of second-degree murder.

teenager who had a history of disruptive behavior and violation of the law. They also pointed to Wendy's tragic childhood
background, as well as the possibility that an overzealous,
overly strict grandmother had physically and psychologically
abused the teenager.

In the end, the jury did not accept Wendy's defense argument. After eleven hours of deliberation, it found her guilty
of second-degree murder. In April 1997, Wendy appeared for
sentencing and was asked by the court for some explanation of
her crime. The crying, frightened teenager, now fifteen, could
not provide a meaningful answer: "Every morning when I
wake up, I look at myself in the mirror, and I can't tell myself I
am a murderer. From the beginning, I was sorry. I never really
thought any of it would really happen."[21]

Wendy Gardner was sentenced to seven years to life in
prison. She received less than the maximum sentence for her
crime because she had not taken part in the actual murder of
Betty Gardner. She will be eligible for parole on her twenty-
first birthday.

The cases of Andrew DeYoung and Wendy Gardner, like
so many similar incidents of adolescent violence, are pain-
fully tragic. These crimes are brutal, senseless, and appear to
lack an understandable motive. Moreover, teenage perpetrators like DeYoung and Gardner are inherently tragic figures
and unlikely murderers. In so many of these cases, there is
every reason to believe that the perpetrator could have had a
happy, nonviolent, and successful life. There was every indication that these children should have been stable, productive
members of our society. Yet somehow these good kids went
disastrously wrong, and they did so in ways that were extraordinarily vicious and incomprehensible.

Depending on one's point of view, such cases almost always offer circumstances that seem to have played more than a
passing role in the perpetrator's moment of lethal violence.
Arguments based on abuse are frequent; however, they are
often tenuous and are rarely accepted by a jury as mitigating

circumstances for murder. The parents of these murderous teenagers are frequently known to have been loving and supportive individuals, although defense attorneys may try to describe them as overly dominant or abusive adults, even when evidence of such a family environment is amorphous and questionable. In the final analysis, we are unable to know the intimate and complex relationships within any family environment. Perhaps there are motivating factors hidden away in the dark, closed closets of many families of teenage murderers. Perhaps there are not.

So much is not understood about why these good kids resort to such horrible acts of violence. Unlike teenagers who rage out of control and murder in a fury, adolescents like Andrew DeYoung and Wendy Gardner kill in a different way—a way that seems especially cold-blooded and calculating. However, like those perpetrators who murder in a rage, these teenagers are often unable to provide a rational reason for their actions, even long after they have committed murder. If they cannot truly understand why they have murdered, can we?

NOTES

1. Peter Verburg, "Rebels without Consciences," *Alberta Report/Western Report* (Internet Edition), 1 May 1995.

2. Ibid.

3. Nicole Schiavi, "Police: Teen's Urge Led Him to Kill Boy for No Good Reason," *San Francisco Chronicle/Associated Press* (Internet Edition), 3 October 1997.

4. Ibid.

5. "Teen 'In a Rut' in Four Murders," *San Francisco Examiner* (Internet Edition), 15 January 1997.

6. Duff Wilson, "Suspect Was Tied to an Earlier Assault," *Seattle Times* (Internet Edition), 16 January 1997.

7. Susan Byrnes, "Gothic Club Ousted Teen Slaying Suspect," *Seattle Times* (Internet Edition), 13 January 1997.

8. Ibid.

9. Barry Bearak, "Two Teens Held after Man's Body Found in Central Park," *New York Times* (Internet Edition), 24 May 1997.

10. Robert Polner and Margaret Ramirez, "The Killing Field—Lone Man Met End Near Strawberry Fields Lake," *Newsday* (Internet Edition), 25 May 1997.

11. Patricia Hurtado, "A Defense Duel—Battle Lines Being Drawn By Lawyers in Park Slaying," *Newsday* (Internet Edition), 29 May 1997.

12. Bearak.

13. Polner and Ramirez.

14. Denise Levin, "Smart, Violent, a Bad Seed, Say Former Friends of Slaying Suspect," *Las Vegas Sun* (Internet Edition), 29 May 1997.

15. Ibid.

16. "Affidavit: Teen Confessed to Girl's Assault, Murder," *Las Vegas Sun* (Internet Edition), 3 June 1997.

17. Levin.

18. "Suspect Arrested in Casino Slaying," *Las Vegas Sun* (Associated Press report, Internet Edition), 29 May 1997.

19. Caren Benjamin, "Teenager Says He Is Innocent in Girl's Slaying," *Las Vegas Review-Journal* (Internet Edition), 26 August 1997.

20. Don Plummer, "Cobb Man Goes on Trial in 3 Slayings," *Atlanta Journal* (Internet Edition), 25 September 1995.

21. Michael Hill, "Just Do It: Last Word Became Last Rites for Doomed Grandmother," *Associated Press* (Internet Edition), 13 April 1997.

5

THE QUESTION OF CONSCIENCE

> The one thing that doesn't abide by majority rule is a person's conscience.
>
> Harper Lee
> *To Kill a Mockingbird*

How do we determine the role of the conscience in an obviously brutal and apparently senseless act of murder? How do we interpret the actions of a violent adolescent who has murdered because of an uncontrollable rage and then deeply regrets his crime? In many cases of adolescent homicide there is no convincing evidence of premeditation, so how can we determine the actual state of mind of the young perpetrator at the moment he lashed out against his victim? Are these teenagers who have so viciously (and apparently so easily) taken another life actually individuals without consciences? Were they born bad and destined to be cold-blooded killers, or are there other factors that overwhelmed their consciences and led them to murder?

In our legal system, such difficult, perhaps ultimately impossible, questions are entrusted to a judge and jury collectively, at least in the case of adult offenders. However, when the defendant is tried as a juvenile, these critical determinations often rest with a single individual—the judge who hears the adolescent's case.

To appreciate the overwhelming difficulties faced by a judge hearing such complex issues, consider the 1996 case of a teenager named "Jon" (who cannot be identified). Fortunately, unlike the judge, we will not be required to make a determination about Jon's fate; nor will we be required to decide any of the other complex issues that regularly confront judges who hear juvenile cases such as this. We will only seek to answer a simple but vital question—a key question about conscience. Did Jon deliberately plan to murder his mother and then carry out his plan in such a way that he was able to completely disregard his conscience? In essence, we are asking if Jon is a ruthless, cold-blooded killer and therefore deserving of harsh, perhaps lethal, punishment. If he is not that, then what is he, and why did he kill?

Facts of the Case. On a hot, sultry summer afternoon in California, Jon presented himself to police officers at a station near his home, confessing that he had murdered his mother earlier that day. According to his confession, Jon had put plugs into his ears, retrieved a .38-caliber handgun that was already in the home, and shot his mother at near point-blank range in the head while she was sitting alone at the family table. At the time of his confession, Jon was fifteen years old. The teenager gave a detailed description of his crime to officers; when asked why he had murdered his mother, he told the interrogators only that he wished he had killed her when he was nine or ten years old. For that, Jon could give no specific reasons. He only repeated to officers that he wished he had committed the crime at a younger age, when he would have received a much lighter punishment.

Officers were immediately dispatched to Jon's home, where they found his mother—a woman in her early fifties—dead from a single gunshot wound to the forehead. The scene was exactly as Jon had described it, and he was immediately charged with murder. Since the murder, Jon has been held in a juvenile detention facility awaiting his trial. The teenager had no criminal record and no history of violence before the murder of his mother. He had lived with her, alone, with no other adult or sibling in the household.

Prosecution Case. The case for the prosecution is strong and simple. Jon confessed to the crime without reservation and not under duress. He claimed that he had considered murdering his mother for years (thereby confirming premeditation) and provided no specific motivation for his action that could be considered mitigating. Despite the absence of any criminal record and a nonviolent history, Jon's actions therefore indicated a crime of premeditated (first-degree) murder. Moreover, the perpetrator showed no remorse to authorities for having murdered his mother. There is no evidence of psychological impairment that could have contributed to Jon's actions, nor are there signs of alcohol or drug use.

Prosecutors were able to locate at least one witness, another teenager, who claimed that he saw and spoke with Jon just before and again just after the murder of his mother. From the statements of this witness, Jon apparently openly declared his intention to kill his mother, left his friend's presence to do so, and returned shortly thereafter, showing no remorse and confirming that he had just committed the act.

On the basis of all these factors, it is the prosecution's position that Jon committed premeditated murder and should be tried as an adult for his crime.

Defense Case. Jon's lawyers do not believe that his crime was premeditated or without remorse; they deny that this is a case of first-degree murder. They point out a number of mitigating circumstances that need to be considered in determining their client's fate.

When Jon was a year old, the woman he murdered many years later adopted him. Jon's attorneys point to the fact that his adoptive mother was a strict disciplinarian, who often told the boy he was worthless and bad. Moreover, his mother raised Jon in a peculiar way, including making her son wash her in the bathtub until he was ten years old and urging him to have fantasy conversations with biblical figures, such as Moses and King David.

Jon's defense team offers the portrait of a young teenager who had been abused psychologically and perhaps physically from a very young age, who then reached a violent breaking point that he could not resist. Based on this scenario, Jon's act of murder was the only way he could free himself from a childhood of horrors. To worsen the situation of Jon's early years, the defense team also brings forward the fact that his natural mother was a mentally ill transient who had a severe drug-abuse problem, thereby possibly predisposing her son to violent behavior.

Finally, the defense team explains Jon's statements to his friends about murdering his mother (as well as his apparent lack of remorse) as the predictable false bravado of a young, teenage male surrounded by his peers, other males, or authority figures.

The defense position is that Jon did murder his mother but that the act was one of desperation involving compelling mitigating circumstances. They argue that their client showed great remorse by voluntarily surrendering to authorities and that he should be remanded to the juvenile court system, where he will receive proper rehabilitation efforts if he is found guilty of the crime. In essence, the defense argues that Jon is a good kid with a fully developed conscience and appropriate sense of the law who committed an atrocious act because he saw no other option to the continuing domination and abuse of his mother.

How are we to interpret such contradictory positions in the context of Jon's conscience? Certainly, only a foolish person would disagree that Jon committed a brutal, egregious act against his mother. Murder is simply not a solution to any problem, and Jon's violence is not acceptable in society. However, that is not the question before us. Our question is one that goes to the heart of the state of mind of an adolescent who kills a parent, family member, or friend: what did Jon *feel* just before he shot his mother at point-blank range? What was his reaction *after* the crime? Why did he make statements to authorities that indicated no remorse for his crime? Did he plan this awful crime and then simply carry it out without regard to right and wrong?

Arguing for the presence of conscience is the fact that Jon surrendered himself shortly after he committed the crime and that he withheld nothing in his confession. Like so many other teenage murderers, Jon could not provide any mitigating circumstances—any excuses—for his actions, and he made no effort to invent any. Certainly, from one point of view this is convincing evidence of remorse and therefore evidence of the presence of conscience. The teenager *acted* as if he was truly sorry for what he had done, even though his *statements* to police seemed to contradict those actions.

Of course, one could argue that Jon was terrified of the consequences of what he had done and felt there were no other options but surrender. However, as demonstrated by other cases in this book, many teenagers make attempts to hide their crimes or flee before they are apprehended or later surrender themselves. In Jon's case, there was no effort to hide his crime or flee from the consequences. Rather, the teenager behaved in a foolhardy way to officers that many would interpret as a complete lack of remorse for what he did. He not only turned himself in as if he was proud of what he had done but complained to police that he had waited too long in his life to commit murder. Certainly, one could argue that this is evidence of an adolescent without a conscience—a teenager devoid of an appropriate understanding of the value of life.

If Jon had a conscience that would otherwise have prohibited him from acting violently, what happened to it at the moment he shot his mother? Certainly, throughout his life before the murder this teenager had behaved as if he cherished life. He did not resort to violence, did not break the law, and was not known as an aggressive, reckless individual. In short, Jon's behavior before the murder would lead a rational individual to believe that he had the capacity of a developed conscience.

Jon's defenders would say that he "snapped." They would claim that so many years of psychological abuse (and perhaps physical abuse) had created a rage in Jon that overwhelmed him and drove him to the point of murder. It was this long period of pain, frustration, growing anger, fear, and desire to be free of a domineering mother that suddenly erupted in a moment of incredible fury that was wholly foreign to Jon's entire existence. These, the defense would argue, are clearly mitigating circumstances: the conditions under which Jon lived inexorably led him to a point at which conscience was not even a consideration—only survival and freedom from pain.

Those who cannot accept such an argument may counter that a person with a fully developed conscience—an individual who truly values the meaning of life—can never put aside a lifetime of beliefs in a moment of rage and mayhem. In addition, there is evidence that Jon may have often disregarded his conscience, at least in relation to his apparent deep hatred for his mother. All one must do is recall the testimony of Jon's friend before and after the murder; surely, they would argue, this is evidence of a sustained disregard for conscience and evidence of obvious premeditation.

In the final analysis, we are no closer to an answer to the question of Jon's conscience than when we began this case. There are so many possibilities for misunderstanding and misinterpretation in such situations. At a minimum, we are adults, and we therefore view the world much differently than individuals like Jon. We view a middle-aged mother with different eyes than her son. We see the ramifications of our actions with greater clarity than a teenager, yet sometimes with a narrowness that often accompanies advancing years.

We know and understand that statements of foolhardy bravado, whether intentional or not, are rarely in our best interest. And yes, we may even understand the priceless value of life more completely and with greater passion than any teenager. However, we are still adults and Jon is still an angry, confused, complex, and murderous teenager. How can we hope to ever understand the forces that drove him to do what he did? Or, if he planned such a crime for a long period of time and brooded over the possibilities of being free of his mother, how can we adequately explain his actions and statements after committing the crime?

Did Jon have a conscience? The answer is both "yes" and "no." It depends entirely on how one interprets his actions and behavior. We cannot know. We can only formulate a belief in one position or the other, or perhaps a third. Unfortunately, as adults, to discern the truth here is not a knowledge or skill we yet possess. We can only be thankful that we are not the judges who hear such cases and who are compelled to try to answer such unanswerable questions. It is clear that when such issues need to be addressed, if we are to err, it must be on the side of life—if we care to be true to our own consciences.

CONSCIENCE—A QUESTION OF COMPROMISE?

For mankind, the search for the essence and meaning of conscience is an ancient one. From the time our forefathers' thoughts and activities first turned to religion, ethics, and philosophy, we have struggled as a species to define conscience and come to an understanding of its role in our individual lives as well as in society. Once the exclusive domain of religion and philosophy, the interpretation of conscience also came to be a topic of particular interest to behaviorists, psychologists, and psychiatrists in the past century and a half. However, despite the long history of our efforts to understand the nature and role of conscience, it remains a very complex and personal issue for each of us.

From a philosophical point of view, we can define conscience as our personal awareness of moral or ethical conduct, which is accompanied by an inner urge to do what we view as right and avoid what we believe to be wrong. It is an inner guide to morality and behavior that directs us to conform to our own sense of right conduct. At its root, this urge to do right is deeply personal and unique for each of us, although there are many issues in any society that benefit from a moral consensus of conscience.

A behaviorist, psychologist, or psychiatrist who leans toward a Freudian view of the psyche would probably define conscience much differently than a philosopher or cleric. He or she would say that conscience is a fundamental part of our superego, which has a very specific role to play in the life and functioning of our psyche. According to Freudian theory, the superego is the part of the psyche that is formed and developed through our acceptance and internalization of the moral standards given us by our parents, other influential people in our lives, and society in general. It is the role of the superego to inform, censor, and restrain the sometimes outlandish and immoral impulses of our ego. Therefore, the superego passes judgement on the ethical or moral nature of our thoughts and actions. The superego passes judgement on what we think, say, or do and sends its evaluation to our ego, where we then consider whether or not we are going to act according to what the superego, our conscience, has advised.

There are of course as many different interpretations of conscience as there are philosophers, religious beliefs, and individuals. However, despite these differences there is an inherent understanding of the role and meaning of conscience that is shared by most humans, even if the importance of its whispered advice is subject to wild variations in interpretation. The majority of us understand conscience as an inevitable and accepted, lifelong companion. Unless we are one of the unfortunate and rare individuals who apparently have no functional conscience whatsoever, a true sociopath, we accept this ever-vigilant censor of our thoughts and deeds as routinely as we assume the next breath or heartbeat. However, as individuals, we each choose to listen more or less attentively to its advice, and we are certainly able to override its recommendations when we feel it is important to do so. By any reasonable definition, scientific or otherwise, it seems that the role of our conscience is always subject to compromise at a deeply personal level.

If we accept this interpretation of conscience (which is certainly no more or less valid than any other), we must consider the conscience as an evolving, developing part of our psyche, much like a personal journal filled with blank pages at birth. In this view, the pages of our personal "journal" are written from our observations and our interactions with parents, guardians, important figures in our lives, and the mores we gather from society. The majority of us instinctively collect the moral and ethical information we need to develop a personal conscience that reflects the knowledge we have gathered. We then make this information a fundamental part of our psyche by the acceptance and codification of ethical and moral considerations by which we try to live our lives. Most of this important work is accomplished at an unconscious level, so long as there is no significant conflict between the developing conscience and our own behavior.

As the pages of our personal journal of conscience become more complete and refined, its role in our lives typically becomes more obvious and compelling. As we develop and mature, our consciences are able to make more frequent and finely tuned judgements about our thoughts, speech, and behavior. We find that we are increasingly subjected to the subtle voice of conscience about many, if not most, of our important activities. We also discover that the urges provided by our conscience are often in conflict with the desires of our ego. Because of this, we learn the art of compromise with ourselves. Over time, the advice of our conscience and the desires of our ego create an internal battlefield on which we arbitrate our ultimate decisions through the exercise of compromise.

If one accepts this view of conscience as feasible and reasonable, two critical issues arise when it is applied to the question of why good kids kill:

- Do these children have consciences, or are they somehow aberrant individuals, born without the capability to develop a fundamental sense of right and wrong?
- If they do have consciences, why was its vital role in their lives so silent and impotent as to be unable to prevent them from killing?

These are troubling questions, and they go to the heart of understanding why good kids kill.

BORN PREDATORS?

Are good kids who commit murder born without consciences? Or are they born with a fully functional personal journal of conscience upon which little or nothing was ever inscribed? Are there other, less simple possibilities that can explain the actions of these adolescents? In any case, the essential question remains the same: how can these good kids commit such atrocities in complete disregard of conscience?

Since they are, by the common definition, "good kids," it seems inconceivable that these teenagers were simply born bad. There is no evidence to support this contention, just as there is no evidence that the majority of these teenagers suffer from anything resembling antisocial personality disorder. None of the teenagers cited in this book had engaged in patterns of illegal, violent, or even significantly negative behavior throughout their young lives. Virtually none of them had a history of violence or conflict with the law. It is inconceivable that these adolescents were born bad and simply did not actuate their true, evil natures until a particular and crucial moment in time. For these adolescents—even those who committed the most heinous crimes—there is little or no evidence that they lacked a fundamentally sound upbringing, which included an appropriate sense of right and wrong. Until they committed murder, these teenagers apparently had a working, functional conscience that was able to direct them toward morally sound decisions whenever it was needed.

Many of these good kids who went so terribly wrong exhibited strong and sincere indications of remorse, thereby persuading us that they were not merely callous sociopaths. Most of them genuinely grieved over their actions, clearly regretted the violence that they had committed, and sincerely wished that none of it had ever happened. A large percentage of these adolescents were unable to explain adequately why they killed yet exhibited profound remorse and declared their general abhorrence for aggression and violence, including their own egregious actions. In the overwhelming majority of these cases, the teenagers clearly demonstrated that they had had a conscience throughout their lives but were still able to disregard their inner voice and commit a vicious murder.

How could this happen? Is the essential issue a catastrophic moral dilemma with some of our children that results in a flagrant disregard for the value of life, or is it something more pervasive but less sinister? Could so many of our children have simply compromised their consciences out of existence?

Certainly, there is a monumental difference between an individual who ignores his or her conscience and engages in petty cheating on a tax return and a person who takes another's life in a wanton act of violence. Obviously, there is a matter of degree that significantly distinguishes these two actions. However, few among us would deny that minor cheating on a tax return is essentially wrong; it is an action that is generally understood to be unethical in our society, and it is against the law. However, it is also an act that is generally overlooked in our society, because it is subject to an easy compromise within the privacy of an individual's code of ethics. In fact, there are so many arguments to be made to justify such minor cheating that for many the admittedly unethical act easily overrides the urging of conscience. In other words, this kind of cheating is wrong, but it is not considered by most Americans to be morally significant. Rather, it is viewed as a simple compromise with conscience that carries little or no enduring moral weight.

However, for most of us there is a tremendous reluctance to wantonly harm another individual. This is a matter of both personal and social conscience that is well understood and clearly defined. For the great majority of our citizens there is no question that murder is immoral and wrong; it is not a debatable issue, and it is not subject to compromise, even if we may fantasize about it as a form of retribution from time to time. Most of us would simply be unable to override the strict imposition of conscience when considering the possibility of killing another human being. Even if one could be guaranteed to be free from recrimination or prosecution for an act of murder, few of us would change our view and disregard our consciences.

Or would we?

In fact, there are individuals for whom this kind of normally unquestioned moral ethic apparently does not exist. For a few, there is no whispered voice of conscience to guide their thoughts, speech, or activities. In our society, these individuals are the sociopaths, with the severe, mostly incurable psychological disease known as antisocial personality disorder. For those who suffer from it, there is no censorship on their behavior and nothing to hold them back from exercising even the most horrible fantasies of violence that may have invaded their minds and captured their desires. These are the members of our society whom we categorize as being without conscience. Their incredibly aggressive, violent, and callous behavior makes them easily recognized and deeply feared.

Medical professionals and those in the behavioral sciences disagree about whether a sociopath is born or made. There are strong arguments that point to a propensity for violent antisocial behavior arising from certain organic deficiencies that existed from birth. There are equally strong arguments for the theory that we create sociopaths within our own families and in society. In fact, even if many cases of antisocial personality disorder are eventually understood to derive from genetic or organic causes, there is little question that environment also plays a large (if not overwhelming) part in the eventual development of a sociopath. Since environment will always play at least some role in the evolution of antisocial behavior, we as parents cannot be absolved of some responsibility for the future violent behavior of our children.

Whatever the genesis of such a disease as antisocial personality disorder, its presence is usually apparent from a young age. The deteriorating, chaotic, unusually callous behavior of a child who may later develop into an aggressive and violent sociopath has a pattern recognizable to psychologists and psychiatrists. Antisocial personality disorder does not suddenly appear in the teenage years and culminate in a quick series of atrocious crimes; a sociopath has a long, identifiable, and somewhat predictable history of aberrant behavior, characterized by a blatant disregard for the rights and safety of others that escalates over time into increasingly aggressive activities.

Certainly, the patterned and troubled history of someone suffering from antisocial personality disorder is not applicable to good kids who kill. By our own social definitions and common understanding, these teenagers would not be categorized as good kids in the first place if they met such troubling behavioral criteria. None of the young murderers discussed in this book were born bad. None of them were sociopaths, as we have come to understand the term. It is likely that each of them had a functional conscience and that each had a well-developed and personal sense of moral propriety. However, they each succumbed to something more powerful than conscience and more overwhelming than any inherent sense of right and wrong. These teenagers murdered because of intense fear and denial, or in a rage that blinded them to anything but the compulsion for retribution, or for other more or less identifiable compulsions. In some cases, they murdered for reasons that no one *yet* understands. However, even in those cases that seem incomprehensible and impossible to explain, there are hints of motivation and there is usually abundant evidence of a functional conscience in the background of the perpetrator, and sometimes overwhelming evidence of intense remorse after the crime.

Are we in the midst of a generation of teenagers who were born predators? Assuredly not. Sadly, we are experiencing a general withdrawal from family and parental responsibilities, and a disturbing new view that labels moral guidance as largely passé and unnecessary in contemporary society. Many of our citizens seem less than concerned about the personal need for a fully developed conscience and the importance of high moral and ethical standards for themselves or their children. We have come to accept compromise as commonplace in dealing with our (seemingly insignificant) infractions against the strict rules of conscience, and we unconsciously pass this acceptance on to our children. What was once unthinkable is now common and accepted. What was once unconscionable is now a matter of negotiation and compromise. If in turn our children seem less guided by conscience and more compelled by the darker, aggressive parts of the psyche, can we legitimately claim surprise and outrage?

6

THE PUNISHMENT PRIORITY

Distrust everyone in whom the impulse to punish is powerful!

Friedrich Nietzsche
Thus Spake Zarathustra

Between 1985 and 1994, the rate of violent juvenile crime nearly doubled in the United States.[1] This dramatic increase in violence created a wave of concern throughout our nation and in Washington, D.C., which resulted in the rapid establishment of much harsher penalties for juvenile offenders than had ever before been seen in this country. The concerns that prompted tougher legislation at the federal level also resulted in significant changes among the states. According to the National Conference of State Legislators, at least forty states currently allow children aged fourteen or younger to be tried as adults for certain felony offenses.[2] This trend toward trying juveniles as adults and imposing stiffer penalties for their crimes represents a dramatic change in the traditional way that adolescents have been brought into our legal system and made to answer for their crimes.

For example, in October 1997, a twelve-year-old boy was convicted of first-degree murder after he beat a forty-five-year-old man to death with a tire iron and robbed him of his social security check. The boy's trial was held in Odessa, Texas. After the guilty verdict was reached, the presiding judge sentenced the perpetrator to thirty years in prison. With his conviction and sentencing, this child offender became the youngest first-degree murder convict in the history of Texas, a state that was already widely known for its tough approach to juvenile crime and harsh sentencing of convicted felons.

However, it should be pointed out that the Odessa case is not typical of the approach taken by most other states in dealing with juvenile lawbreakers. Historically, the American judicial system has tended to direct violent teenage offenders into the juvenile court system, where if found guilty of their crimes, the individuals would not be intermingled with adult offenders and could benefit from attempts at rehabilitation. However, in recent years there has been a sustained and pervasive effort to bring violent adolescents to trial as adults and bypass the juvenile court system.

The widespread increase in violent juvenile crime and the often-heinous nature of the criminal acts have caused fear, anger, and outrage across this country. Such incidents as the one that occurred in Jonesboro, Arkansas, in March 1998, in which four children and a teacher were gunned down by two boys of only eleven and thirteen leave us stunned and disbelieving at the deep level of violence in America. Moreover, these horrific acts seem to be increasing as evidenced by teenage schoolyard murder sprees in Pearl, Mississippi, in October 1997 and in Paducah, Kentucky, only two months later. In each of these incidents, multiple victims were claimed by young shooters who were driven to senseless and inexplicable violence. Understandably, legislators at all levels have been encouraged by their constituents to take a much tougher stance on juvenile crime. In most cases, this mandate is interpreted as a need for the imposition of stiffer penalties and a narrowing of the historical view that crimes committed by teenagers are fundamentally different than crimes committed by adults.

Many juveniles (some as young as fourteen or fifteen years old) who are not sent through the juvenile court system have committed crimes of such a gruesome and disturbing nature that there is a reluctance on the part of judges to do anything but have them tried as adults. Certainly, such legal decisions are difficult ones and may often be motivated by sensitivity to local politics, at least in the cases of many elected officials and judges. However, regardless of the motivations for trying a teenager as an adult, one cannot dismiss the significant impact of the crime itself on the opinions and attitudes of any judge, legislator, jury member, or citizen.

For example, in October 1993, at the age of fifteen, Gerard McCra brutally murdered his parents and eleven-year-old sister by shooting them to death. Like so many other murderous teenagers, McCra had no prior criminal record or history of violence. However, before he committed the murders McCra had argued with his parents because they had steadfastly refused to allow him to sleep with his girlfriend in the McCra family home. In a rage of anger, the young teenager murdered his entire family and then had repeated sex with his girlfriend, who was unaware of the bodies lying in a nearby room of the house. Despite his young age at the time of the murders, McCra was tried as an adult before a jury, found guilty of three counts of first-degree murder, and sentenced to life in prison.

In February 1997, two brothers plotted and carried out the murder of their parents because the elder brother was angry about the way their parents had reacted to his poor grades in school. Robert Dingman, seventeen years old, later claimed he had been furious because his parents imposed a curfew and

---

Snapshot Profile of Gerard McCra

A fifteen-year-old high school student without any criminal record or history of violence. For reasons he was never able to adequately explain, McCra murdered both parents and his eleven-year-old sister in an uncontrolled rage, apparently because he was forbidden to sleep with his girlfriend in the family home.

refused to buy him a cellular phone until he improved his deteriorating grades. Together with his brother, fifteen-year-old Jeffrey, he made a plan to murder their parents. On the afternoon of February 6, 1997, Robert shot his parents repeatedly with a .22-caliber handgun. After the murders, and with the help of his younger brother, Dingman wrapped the victims' bodies in plastic and hid them in the attic of their New Hampshire family home.

The murders were soon discovered, and Jeffrey Dingman was persuaded to testify against his older brother in exchange for a guilty plea to a reduced charge of second-degree murder. Robert Dingman was charged with first-degree murder and tried as an adult before a jury. The trial took two weeks, and then the jury took four days to reach a verdict. When it was announced, Robert Dingman was found guilty of first-degree murder and sentenced to life in prison without the possibility of parole. His brother, Jeffrey, received a sentence of eighteen to thirty years in prison in exchange for his plea bargain.

Acts of horrific violence, like those committed by Gerard McCra, shock and frighten all who learn of them. This is particularly true because the offender, a teenager, is often an unlikely murderer. Because these crimes generate such a strong

Snapshot Profiles of
Robert and Jeffrey Dingman

Two teenage brothers who had no histories of violence or criminal activities. The elder brother, Robert, was angry with his parents because they had imposed a curfew and refused to buy him a cellular phone after he received poor grades at school. Together with his younger brother, Jeffrey, Robert murdered their parents. At trial, Jeffrey testified against his brother and received a prison sentence of eighteen to thirty years. Robert received a sentence of life in prison without the possibility of parole.

and widespread emotional reaction, it is not surprising that legislators, members of the legal profession, and most citizens react with outrage and a focused determination to severely punish the perpetrator, regardless of his or her age.

A STRONG LEGISLATIVE RESPONSE

For the past two decades, federal and state legislators have given a great deal of attention to strengthening existing penalties applicable to violent juvenile crime. Much of the new and tougher legislation at the federal level is in direct response to a general concern among American citizens that youthful violent crime is out of control in this country. The steady increase in juvenile crime is deeply troubling and comes at a time when violent crime in general has decreased somewhat. There is also a widespread belief that juvenile crime is likely to become even more of a significant national problem in the next decade as many of our children enter their adolescent years.

In recent years many states have also enacted much stiffer legislation designed to deter adolescent violent crime by the imposition of stricter penalties, which usually take the form of forcing juvenile offenders to be tried as adults. The majority of states have passed laws designed to make it easier to try juveniles as adults, even at a very young age. More than a dozen states now routinely deal with juveniles who commit violent crimes as adults, and most states no longer expunge the criminal records of juveniles when they become eighteen years old.

Most of the legislation that has emanated from the federal level in recent years is clear in its intent to stiffen the penalties for juveniles who have committed a violent crime. In general, such legislation has two primary objectives: (1) increase the number of juveniles who can be tried as adults for their crimes, and (2) enhance the penalties for such crimes. Unfortunately, in many cases this legislation has not adequately addressed effective crime prevention methodologies or such critical issues as incarcerating teenagers in prisons that house adult, career criminals. However, these new laws seem to reflect accurately the mood of the nation.

As early as 1985, the United States Congress focused its efforts on the issue of violent juvenile crime. In that year the Young Offenders Act was passed, which dealt specifically with crimes committed by juveniles between the ages of twelve and eighteen. In essence, this act provided that a child under twelve could not be charged with a criminal offense, while a teenager over the age of seventeen would be subject to all adult criminal law provisions. The point of the Young Offenders Act was to strike a balance between punishment and rehabilitation for juvenile offenders. It featured such provisions as shorter prison sentences in exchange for community service and the protection of the offender's identity when he or she became an adult. However, this act did not meet the expectations and growing concern of citizens and legislators as the trend in violent crimes committed by our children continued to escalate throughout the remainder of the 1980s and into the 1990s.

In 1994 Congress passed legislation entitled the Violent Crime Control and Law Enforcement Act of 1994. The point of this act was to strengthen the existing laws applicable to violent juvenile crime and stiffen the methods of punishing adolescent offenders. This legislation significantly enhanced the ability of prosecutors to try juveniles as adults. Among the key points of the act were:

• A reduction in the age, from fifteen to thirteen years, at which juveniles could be tried as adults for certain violent crimes in which a firearm was used.

• The ability to try sixteen- and seventeen-year-old juveniles as adults for (1) first- and second-degree murder, (2) attempted murder, (3) armed robbery in which a firearm was used, (4) aggravated battery or assault when a firearm was used, (5) criminal sexual penetration when armed with a firearm, and (6) drive-by shootings.

- Substantial increase in the penalties for employing children to distribute drugs near schools and playgrounds.
- A general increase in the penalties for juveniles found guilty of violent crimes.

Three years after this act was passed, in April 1997, the House of Representatives Judiciary Committee approved a bill that would require the federal government to try *most* juvenile offenders, even those as young as thirteen years old, as adults. Although the bill received some strong criticism, especially from House Democrats, the committee passed it by a 14–9 vote. In addition to establishing new and stronger federal mandates, the bill encouraged states to try most juveniles as young as fifteen years old as adults by offering a $1.5 billion package of grants to help finance state court systems, salaries for probation officers, and the construction of new jails. The clear intent of the bill was to strongly address the continuing national concern about the increase in serious crimes committed by adolescents. However, there was considerable disagreement about whether such a tactic was proper and wise or primarily an exercise in politics. In any case, the bill did not provide specific crime prevention measures but almost exclusively dealt with punishing juvenile offenders.

Less than two weeks later, the House of Representatives passed the bill by a 286–132 majority. Commenting on the strong support for this bill and its potential impact on juvenile crime, Representative George Gekas (Republican from Pennsylvania) noted that it would treat young offenders "as the predators they seem to be."[3] However, some members of Congress, like Representative John Conyers (Democrat from Michigan) strongly disagreed with this sentiment and with the bill itself: "The only thing left is an amendment abolishing the distinction between children and adults."[4]

That there is a strong and popular national outcry to protect American citizens against the very real threat of violent juvenile crime is obvious. This fear-driven reaction is understandable and genuine. Violent crime committed by teenagers is an overwhelming problem in this country and threatens to become epidemic in the decades ahead. However, it is vital that any legislation designed to address the legitimate issue of offender punishment balance this objective with the essential goal of crime prevention. To do anything less is to deal with this critical issue only *after* a violent crime has been committed and without regard to the possibilities of preventing it in the first place. The often-heard argument that stiffer punishments for violent juvenile crime are adequate to reduce the incidents of future violence has already proven dubious or false in the case of adult offenders. It is unlikely that our national experience will be different when dealing with juvenile offenders.

A GROWING COMMITMENT TO TOUGH PROSECUTION

With strong support from federal legislators and the public in general, a renewed commitment to the prosecution of violent juvenile crime has become manifest across America. Increasingly state prosecutors, legislators, and ordinary citizens have demanded that adolescent offenders be tried and sentenced as adults, even though most agree that it is unwise to routinely jail convicted teenagers with adult offenders. In great measure, this movement toward stiffening the punishments imposed on juvenile offenders is in reaction to the often gruesome and horrific nature of many of the homicides committed by our children. In part, this reaction is due to the intense media coverage that persistently surrounds this issue.

The tenacity shown by prosecutors of violent juveniles is sometimes amazing and occasionally controversial. This was true in the case of Melissa Garrison, a fifteen-year-old who was tried four times for murder as an adult before she was finally convicted.

In 1992, Betty Garrison, a forty-five-year-old social worker and the mother of two girls, was murdered in her home before dawn. The attack on Garrison was especially brutal and disturbing. The woman was stabbed repeatedly, smothered, and strangled in her own bedroom. Incredibly, her two daughters and another teenager had attacked and killed her. Shannon Garrison, 17, Melissa Garrison, 15, and Allen Robert Goul, 15, admitted to the murder of Betty Garrison. Goul was Melissa's boyfriend at the time of the crime. None of the teenagers were able to provide a reasonable motive for the crime, nor did any of the perpetrators demonstrate remorse for their actions. In addition, the murder had been planned in advance and well orchestrated. The two teenage girls had held Mrs. Garrison down and smothered her while Goul stabbed the terrified woman to death.

All three teenagers were charged with murder, and prosecutors in the case demanded that they be tried as adults. Realizing that they had little or no chance of winning their cases at trial, Shannon Garrison and Allen Goul both pleaded guilty to murder in 1993 and received life sentences in prison. However, Melissa Garrison did not plead guilty. Rather, she opted to present her case before a jury, claiming that she did not actively take part in the murder of her mother.

Melissa Garrison's case was a complex one, made even more confusing by the fact that the teenager often contradicted herself when speaking about her role in the murder. Nonetheless, she was determined to have her day in court.

Over the next few years, Garrison was tried on four separate occasions for the charge of murder. Her first three trials

---

Snapshot Profile of Melissa Garrison

A fifteen-year-old who participated in the murder of her mother along with her boyfriend and older sister in 1992. The teenager was tried on four separate occasions (as an adult) for the crime before she was eventually found guilty of murder. She is now serving a life sentence in prison.

ended in hung juries; with each incomplete verdict, prosecutors in the case publicly announced their intention to try the teenager again. The tenacity of the prosecutors was hailed by many as appropriate, but it was condemned by others as a waste of time and the taxpayers' money. Nonetheless, there was no limit to the commitment by officials to have the Garrison trial reach some kind of definitive verdict. Finally, in 1994, Melissa Garrison's fourth trial resulted in a guilty verdict after only a little more than three hours of deliberation. The presiding judge in the case subsequently sentenced the teenager to life in prison.

Although this level of tenacity is not common among prosecutors of cases of juvenile crimes, it is indicative of a growing commitment to have teenage offenders face the same rigors and potential punishments as adult offenders. Increasingly throughout this country, prosecutors are insisting on directing young offenders away from the juvenile court system and into the adult offender system. In many, perhaps most, areas of the United States, this tough approach to violent juvenile crime receives wide and strong public support, even when the question is one of life or death for the adolescent offender.

THE DEATH PENALTY

Our nation has a long and unhappy history of executing adolescents for violent crimes—a history that extends back to the seventeenth century and continues to the present day. In 1642, a Plymouth Colony boy of sixteen, Thomas Graunger, was hanged for having sex with a horse and a cow. The youngest person ever executed in the United States was ten-year-old James Arcene. This child was hanged in Arkansas in 1885 after being convicted of murder and robbery. Since the beginning of this century, the youngest person executed in the United States was Fortune Ferguson, Jr., who was put to death in 1927. Ferguson had been convicted of raping an eight-year-old girl when he was thirteen. However, despite these extreme examples, the American system of justice has traditionally not been quick to execute juveniles, even though such a sentence is carried out in this country if the crime is viewed as especially egregious.

In the past decade, the United States Supreme Court handed down two important decisions that redefined our use of the death penalty in cases of adolescent homicide. In 1988, the Court heard the case of *Thompson v. Oklahoma*, in which the constitutionality of executing an individual under the age of sixteen was at issue. The fundamental question before the Court was whether or not such an execution would constitute cruel and unusual punishment, thereby violating a key provision of the Eighth Amendment to the U.S. Constitution. The case involved a fifteen-year-old, William Wayne Thompson, who had committed a premeditated murder in January 1983. Thompson's guilt was not at issue. Rather, it was the imposition of the death penalty that caused the case to be heard by the Supreme Court. In a momentous decision, the Court decided that such an execution would in fact violate the Eighth Amendment. Because of this decision, Thompson's life was spared. In one opinion on the case, Justice Sandra Day O'Connor argued that individuals "below the age of sixteen at the time of their offense may not be executed under the authority of a capital punishment statute that specifies no minimum age at which the commission of a capital crime can lead to the offender's execution."[5]

However, only a year later the Supreme Court agreed to hear two other cases that revisited its previous ruling. In 1989, the Court heard the cases of *Stanford v. Kentucky* and *Wilkins v. Missouri*, both of which dealt with an issue similar to that raised by *Thompson v. Oklahoma*. In the 1989 cases the question before the Court was whether or not the execution of a sixteen- or seventeen-year-old offender violated the Eighth Amendment clause that dealt with cruel and unusual punishment. In both the Stanford and Wilkins cases, the perpetrators had been found guilty of murder and, as in the case of William Wayne Thompson, the question of guilt was not at issue. Justice Antonin Scalia summarized the argument made before the Court to set aside the death penalty in these cases:

The thrust of both Wilkins's and Stanford's arguments is that imposition of the death penalty on those who were juveniles when they committed their crimes falls within the Eighth Amendment prohibition against "cruel and unusual punishments." Wilkins would have us define juveniles as individuals sixteen years of age and under; Stanford would draw the line at seventeen.[6]

The conclusion of the Supreme Court was that there was no national consensus against executing sixteen- or seventeen-year-old offenders convicted of murder. Therefore, by a vote of five to four, the Court upheld the right of the states to use capital punishment in such cases. Since these two critical rulings in 1988 and 1989, no decision by the Supreme Court has restrained or diminished the use of capital punishment against juveniles sentenced to death in cases of murder.

In recent decades, a renewed and strengthened belief in the death penalty as a method of crime deterrence has arisen in America. Now, most Americans view this ultimate form of punishment as appropriate for adolescents who commit an especially heinous murder or similarly violent crimes. In fact, since the mid-1970s, a majority of Americans has expressed a growing and vocal support for the death penalty in general. This widespread support has made a clear impression on legislators, who often express their own belief in the death penalty through the creation of new laws and the establishment of increasingly harsh punishments for perpetrators of any violent crime.

In 1994, the governor of Mississippi, Kirk Fordice, announced his intention to make that state "the capital of capital punishment."[7] His comments reflected a strong belief in America that violent crime, especially violent crimes committed by adolescents, was out of control. For many citizens and legislators, the answer to this dilemma was seen to be stiffer punishments and an increased use of the death penalty (see Table 6.1).

By 1997, the state of Mississippi had four juveniles on death row who had committed their crimes while under the age of eighteen. Throughout this country, approximately fifty adolescents were in the same situation at that time. Statistically, this reflected a 39 percent increase in the number of juveniles on death row since 1983. In the twenty years following the 1973 decision of the United States Supreme Court to reinstate the death penalty, nine males have been executed who were under the age of eighteen when they committed their crimes (see Table 6.2).[8]

When one examines the profiles of adolescents currently on death row, we find that about 75 percent of the offenders were seventeen years old when they murdered, while the remainder were sixteen. Two-thirds of these juvenile offenders belonged to a minority group, and all the perpetrators were male. The victims of these offenders were overwhelmingly adults—81 percent. Over half the victims were Caucasian, and about half were females.

One of the most difficult and troubling issues surrounding the death penalty, particularly when it applies to juveniles, is that there are many inconsistencies in the way various states impose this ultimate form of punishment. However, there are some general principles that also seem to apply across most jurisdictions. For example, in those states that have the death penalty available as an option, a juvenile who participated in an act of murder does not necessarily receive the death penalty if he or she did not directly cause the death of the victim.

Twenty-one states currently impose a minimum age of sixteen for the death penalty, while four others impose a minimum age of seventeen (see Table 6.3). Twelve states are without the death penalty (Alaska, Hawaii, Iowa, Maine, Massachusetts, Michigan, Minnesota, North Dakota, Rhode Island, Vermont, West Virginia, and Wisconsin).

Because of recent changes in legislation at the federal level, many states are now reviewing their judicial and penal policies and considering lowering the minimum age at which a juvenile can be tried as an adult and executed for a capital offense. Without question, there is a growing movement across this nation to make greater use of the ultimate punishment, and many states, like Mississippi, may also soon opt to become a "capital of capital punishment," in an effort to stem the tide of increasing juvenile violence.

Table 6.1
Number of Executions (all ages) since 1981

YEAR	Number of Executions
1981	1
1982	2
1983	5
1984	21
1985	18
1986	18
1987	25
1988	11
1989	16
1990	23
1991	14
1992	31
1993	38
1994	31
1995	56
1996	45

Table 6.2
Juveniles Executed Between 1973 and 1993 in the U.S.

Name	Year of Execution	Place of Execution	Age at Crime	Age at Execution
Charles Rumbaugh	1985	Texas	17	28
J. T. Roach	1986	South Carolina	17	25
Jay Pinkerton	1986	Texas	17	24
Dalton Prejean	1990	Louisiana	17	30
J. Garrett	1992	Texas	17	28
Curtis Harris	1993	Texas	17	31
F. Lashley	1993	Missouri	17	29
Ruben Cantu	1993	Texas	17	26
C. Burger	1993	Georgia	17	33

Table 6.3
States with Minimum Ages for the Execution of Juveniles

Age 16 Minimum	Age 17 Minimum	Age 18 Minimum
Alabama	Georgia	California
Arizona	New Hampshire	Colorado
Arkansas	North Carolina	Connecticut
Delaware	Texas	Illinois
Florida		Kansas
Idaho		Maryland
Indiana		Nebraska
Kentucky		New Jersey
Louisiana		New Mexico
Mississippi		New York
Missouri		Ohio
Montana		Oregon
Nevada		Tennessee
Oklahoma		
Pennsylvania		
South Carolina		
South Dakota		
Utah		
Virginia		
Washington		
Wyoming		

THE BALANCING ACT

As we stand at the threshold of the new millennium, our society faces a number of challenges that reach deeply into the personal lives of our children and ourselves. There is no question that as individuals we must take proactive measures to reduce the escalation of violent juvenile crime across America. Initially, our reaction to this threat has been to enact tougher legislation designed to bring young offenders to trial as adults and deal with them more harshly. However, in so doing we risk falling into the familiar cycle of ever-increasing punishments and escalating recidivism rates that we have already experienced with traditional adult offenders. Perhaps this is one of the general concepts of the use of punishment that Friedrich Nietzsche had in mind when he penned the phrase (in *Thus Spake Zarathustra*), "Distrust everyone in whom the impulse to punish is powerful!"

However, it is also clear that we cannot allow juvenile offenders, particularly those who commit violent crimes, to go untried and unpunished. To do so would be tantamount to giving ourselves over to anarchy. This is a dilemma of such magnitude that resolving it has become crucial to the safety of future generations in America. If we are to address the challenge of violent juvenile crime, we must do so on a broad basis and with a holistic approach that strives to prevent future violence by future generations.

Despite America's tough posture in dealing with violent crime, our society continues to be victimized by it. Certainly, we must recognize that the punishment priority, although vital, is not sufficient on its own to turn back violent crime in America. This is particularly true with young offenders.

As we bring more and more juveniles into our adult offender system, we run the risk of creating more and more career criminals. Our prison system is already stretched beyond the breaking point with adult offenders. The question of how to incarcerate violent juvenile offenders in our efforts to keep

up with our increasing conviction rate has not yet been satisfactorily answered. This too is a social dilemma that demands
an early resolution.

The role of rehabilitation for violent juvenile offenders is
also unclear and unsettled. For example, after surveying the
case histories in this book, how many of these children would
be likely to repeat their crimes in the future? None of these
adolescents were career criminals. In fact, these were offenders without violent backgrounds or criminal records until they
committed their crimes. None of these teenagers exhibited the
escalating pattern of criminal behavior that we have come to
recognize as the first chapters in the long life of a career criminal. How then do we assess the probabilities of these adolescents becoming violent in the future? Are they likely to do
so, and if so, in what way? Is it possible that most of these
offenders would be excellent candidates for rehabilitation—
adolescents who are unlikely to ever commit a violent crime
again? If they are, then these teenagers are, by definition, good
candidates for rehabilitation and poor candidates for incar-
ceration with violent adult offenders.

These are difficult questions, and they go to the heart of our
proper use of rehabilitation efforts. However, if adolescents
such as most of those described in this book are thrown into
an adult prison, there will be no opportunity for rehabilitation.
There will only be the opportunity to punish and, perhaps,
create another career criminal where there had been none.

This is not to say that the punishments we choose to impose for violent juvenile crime should be meaningless or inap-
propriate. Certainly, many crimes committed by our children
are especially gruesome and callous; such actions against society obviously warrant appropriate punishment. However, we
must always be vigilant that we do not worsen the situation by
creating more opportunities for future violence by failing to
focus on the long-term results of our own judicial actions. If
we do no more than simply lock these offenders away in our
efforts to protect society, we run the risk of future violence by

failing to prepare them as adults to reenter society, which many of them will eventually do. Certainly, this is a harsh lesson that we have already learned through the failures of our adult penal system.

Clearly, the most effective action we can take must involve prevention of violent crime in the first place. However, we cannot look to the judicial or penal systems in America to prevent crime. In the case of youthful offenders, we must look primarily to the family for prevention and intervention. For our children, this is the place of first and best opportunity to learn what is needed to avoid crime and violence. Unfortunately, we have not done as good of a job with our children as we should have, and we are now paying the price for our shortcomings. Without a strong, uncompromising commitment to nonviolence and respect within our families, we cannot expect our children to become better than the standards we set for them. Also, we cannot expect our agencies and institutions to take up the responsibilities that we as parents must rightfully assume.

In the final analysis, if we are to make inroads against the escalating violence of our children, we must fully accept our parental responsibilities, make our children aware of their social responsibilities, and view ourselves as full partners in society rather than as isolated individuals. Beyond this, we must structure our judicial and penal systems in such a way that we avoid creating future criminal behavior where none would have otherwise existed. Where could such an approach be more effective than with our children?

NOTES

1. "Fighting Kid Crime," *USA Today* (Internet Edition), 12 May 1997.

2. Antonio Olivo and Ken Ellingwood, "A Family Torn from Within," *Los Angeles Times Home Edition* (Internet Edition), 29 May 1996.

3. David Judson, "House OKs Bill to Try Kids as Adults," *USA Today* (Internet Edition), 9 May 1997.

4. Ibid.

5. Charles Patrick Ewing, *Kids Who Kill* (New York: Avon Books, 1990), 158–159.

6. Ibid.

7. Stephanie Saul, "Adult Punishment: Minors Face Death Row for Crimes," *Newsday* (Internet Edition), 3 March 1997.

8. Ibid.

HOPE AND CHANGE

It is change, continuing change, inevitable change, that is the
dominant factor in society today.

Isaac Asimov
My Own View

It is more than a little troubling to read about any form of extreme violence, especially when it concerns good kids who
murder in such brutal and senseless ways, as have the teenagers discussed in this book. However, despite the egregious
acts they committed, these adolescents represent an obviously
small minority in our society. Although it is true that we are a
generally violent nation, we are not predominantly so, and our
children are not inherently aggressive and prone to criminality. It is easy to slip into a fear-driven belief that we are at risk
in every avenue of our lives and that our own children lie at
the heart of a large percentage of the violence in America.
In fact, many of our citizens hold an unshakable belief that
our teenagers are far more violent than they really are. For example, a 1994 Gallup poll reported that the average American
adult believed that adolescents committed 43 percent of all
violent crimes in the United States. However, in that same
year, they were actually responsible for only 13 percent of
such crimes.

This is not meant to imply that hardly any of our children
are violent. The truth is that the adolescent population of our
country is more violent now than ever before in our history.
However, this is not a situation for which there is no solution.

There is inherently no reason to believe that we must accept an ever-increasing level of violence by our children and relegate ourselves to the role of helpless and impassive bystanders. Nor can we rely on external agencies such as the government or educational institutions to solve the problem for the rest of us.

If we are to address the challenge of escalating teenage violence, our efforts must begin with our own children, in our own families, and in our own homes. For this process of renewal to begin, each of us must be aware of the nature of adolescent violence and how to recognize its potential warning signs among those closest to us. Armed with this knowledge, we can become proactive in bringing the concepts of nonviolence to our children and in so doing better secure their futures and ours. However, this is a difficult undertaking that by its nature will often be fraught with emotionalism, misunderstanding, and frustration.

PREDICTING ADOLESCENT VIOLENCE

Even recognized experts in adolescent behavior are at a loss to explain many of the shocking and especially brutal murders that are committed by teenagers in this country. Charles Patrick Ewing, Ph.D., author of *Kids Who Kill*, has studied the violence of children for many years yet admits that he cannot begin to predict when adolescent rage will erupt into murder:

You have a kid who kills and you look into her background and say people should have known this was coming. Hindsight is always twenty-twenty. But if you identify one thousand kids who had similar experiences and difficulties at age seven, then follow them through the rest of their lives, most of them won't be killers, they won't be criminals. So it's hard to predict. It may well be that it's inexplicable.[1]

On an individual case basis, this inherent uncertainty is obvious and powerful. There is little on the immediate horizon of the behavioral or criminal sciences that promises to overturn this element of uncertainty. However, on a broader scale, is there hope to predict future violent behavior? Can we look into the future and see what it holds for our children and ourselves? Are we destined to experience an annually increasing level of violent juvenile crime until the very foundations of our society are threatened by it?

In 1997, the RAND Corporation published a briefing paper entitled, "The Coming Wave of Violence in California." This document explored the question of whether California was destined to experience a significant wave of violence perpetrated by the increasing number of children who would enter their teenage years over the next two decades. A briefing was originally presented to the Homicide Research Working Group in June 1996, and it was later committed to written form for wide distribution.

At the heart of the effort to estimate future juvenile violence was the selection of an appropriate model of prediction that would not only account for the changing demographics of California but also make a reasonable estimate of the future annual homicide arrest rate. In their briefing RAND selected three possible scenarios for the future homicide arrest rate:

- A pessimistic assumption that the rate would increase by 3 percent each year
- A nominal assumption that the rate would increase by 1 percent each year
- An optimistic assumption that the rate would decrease by 1 percent each year

The pessimistic assumption was considered to be a reasonable upper bound on projections and the optimistic assumption a reasonable lower bound; the nominal assumption represented the most likely scenario for the future of California. If the nominal assumption proves correct, the arrest rate for homicide in the year 2021 will be 28 percent higher than it is today.

Overall, this seemed to be the most reasonable future vision of teenage violent crime over the next few decades. Certainly, however, such an apparently reasonable prediction did not sound like good news to those who heard the RAND Corporation presentation.

However, the briefing noted two critical points that could greatly influence the future arrest rate: (1) demographic change tends to happen very slowly and is therefore a relatively weak cause of changes in violence, but (2) behavioral change can happen very quickly and can strongly influence changes in violence.[2]

In essence, the RAND Corporation gave reason for hope for both California and the nation. That is, the mere fact that we will experience a burgeoning teenage population in the coming decades does not necessarily imply that violence will rage out of control. In fact, the demographic issue alone would not support such a pessimistic view of our future. As pointed out in the briefing document, behavioral change is a much more important factor in determining the likelihood of future violence, and behavioral change is something within our control:

It is the behavior of the next generation that will largely shape the future. . . . In short, California may face an impending wave of violence, but not an inevitable one. One element in the equation that matters—the future behavior of today's children—is one that could be modified.[3]

Clearly, this puts the ball squarely in our court as parents, adults, and mentors for the next generation—and that is how it should be. If, as implied by the RAND Corporation, we have reason to hope for a less violent future for our children, should we not be responsible for attaining that goal? The answer seems obvious. The challenge lies in determining how to create the behavioral changes in ourselves and our children that will ensure a less violent future. Once again, we must look to the family environment as a starting point for change. However, is this a reasonable and practical place to start?

WHEN ALL THEIR LOVE ISN'T ENOUGH

Despite the best, and sometimes heroic, efforts of parents, nonviolent teenagers can commit brutal, inexplicable crimes of passion. When this kind of tragedy occurs, it becomes even more difficult to understand and accept the outcome: all the love and support of a close family proved insufficient to steer the adolescent from his or her determined, if not intentional, course of lethal violence. The rage, frustration, and hopelessness that such adolescents experience seems to overwhelm the love, trust, and support that surrounds them. Such was the sad case of Brian Tate.

Brian was the sixteen-year-old son of Arthur and Rita Tate, who lived in Maryland. Brian's father was the successful owner of a construction company, and his mother was a technical writer. The family lived in a comfortable home on a wooded lot with their three children. Brian was the oldest.

As he entered his teenage years, Brian showed a special talent for athletics. By his sophomore year in high school the teenager stood six feet tall and was a star on his school football team. Throughout his childhood and into his adolescence Brian had been a stable, polite, and pleasant individual who benefited from a close and loving family environment. He had no criminal record or history of violence.

In 1992, Brian dated a local teenager who claimed she was deeply in love with him. It was obvious to Brian's parents that he too was in love. In February of that year, she abruptly broke off their relationship and began dating another teenager, who was nineteen years old and not in school. Brian was devastated by the loss of his girlfriend and told his mother that he felt he had nothing left to live for. For several months prior to this incident, Rita Tate had noticed some troubling changes in her son. Uncharacteristically, Brian, the high school team's quarterback, had been benched because he had exhibited poor team spirit. At about the same time, his grades began to drop. Throughout the months of the developing emotional crisis that preceded the collapse of his love relationship, the Tates made repeated efforts to provide help for their son. They consulted a therapist, enrolled the teenager in a new school that could provide more personal attention, and remained extremely supportive at home. However, nothing seemed to lift the teenager from his downward emotional spiral. Now Brian had been rejected by his girlfriend; he was deeply hurt and became uncommunicative. To Mrs. Tate it seemed as though Brian was seriously considering suicide, and she was deeply concerned for his welfare.

The weekend after Brian lost his girlfriend, the elder Tates stayed very close to their son, urging him to talk about his feelings and showing as much support as they could. According to Mrs. Tate's characterization of that weekend, "We just sat on him, kept talking to him."[4] At the same time, they placed telephone calls to a local therapist, who never called back. However, Brian never discussed his feelings in detail with his parents.

Snapshot Profile of Brian Tate

A sixteen-year-old from a close, supportive family. He had been a star athlete and successful student until six months before he murdered a rival teenager over a lost girlfriend. In Brian's case, his parents had provided extensive support and tried repeatedly to help their son when he experienced emotional problems. However, despite their efforts, Brian committed a vicious murder that was completely at odds with his nature and upbringing. He was arrested, pleaded guilty to murder, and was sentenced to life imprisonment in a maximum-security prison.

On Monday, February 24, 1992, Brian went to school as usual, took a geometry test, and received an A grade. After school, he went out with a friend, allegedly to buy school supplies. However, when he did not return by ten o'clock that evening, a worried Arthur and Rita Tate went out looking for their son. At the same time his parents were searching for him, Brian was at the house of the teenager who was now dating his ex-girlfriend. He had brutally attacked the nineteen-year-old with brass knuckles and then stabbed him twenty-four times. Even as his rival begged for his life, Brian continued the vicious attack until the nineteen-year-old was dead.

Brian Tate was arrested the next day and charged with murder. While awaiting his trial the teenager was examined by defense psychiatrists and found to be suffering from a number of personality disorders. However, prosecutors rejected these opinions and insisted that the teenager had committed premeditated murder without mitigating circumstances. Brian eventually pleaded guilty to first-degree murder and was sentenced to life in prison at a state maximum-security penitentiary.

In the case of Brian Tate one cannot imagine the pain and sorrow of his parents, or that of the parents of the slain teenager. It is clear from the facts of the case that Brian's parents had been committed to the welfare of their son and willing to take whatever steps were necessary to help him in his time of need. However, despite their extensive efforts, no one was able to reach Brian. The pain, sense of abandonment, and rage that he obviously carried deep within himself led Brian to commit a brutal crime that seemed, certainly to his parents, completely unthinkable and foreign to the child they knew and loved. It is difficult to imagine what else Brian's parents could have done to divert their son from his course of violence. Sadly, this is often the case with teenagers who resort to murder, but it need not always be so.

PARENTS AND THEIR TEENAGERS

When children enter their teenage years, it can often seem to parents as if the entire structure of the family has been suddenly and inexplicably thrown into chaos. The relationships parents have so diligently and carefully structured with their children inevitably undergo immense, confusing, and sometimes painful changes. For the child now entering his or her teenage years, all interpersonal relationships are subject to scrutiny and reevaluation. Many, perhaps most, will be forever transformed, for better or worse. Such abrupt and pervasive changes in the relationships that are fundamental to the family structure can cause tension, misunderstanding, and distrust if parents are not able to adequately understand their fast-growing, evolving teenagers, as well as their own changing roles in the family.

However, the years of adolescence also represent a time of learning and development that can be exciting and profound for both teenager and parents. During these crucial years, adolescents formulate and codify their views of the meaning of life, love, friendship, relationships, and their proper place in the family and in society. This new perspective of the teenager's environment includes a necessary reevaluation of the role of parents. These are trying times for both the adolescent and his parents, because the emerging adult has seemed to move quickly and easily away from everything that his parents have come to rely on. However, this is a natural, inevitable process that can be a time of sharing and learning for both the teenager and his parents. It is during these critical years that a new relationship can be forged with our sons and daughters— a relationship that is even more fulfilling and meaningful than one of a parent with a child. A need for close and traditional parenting, which had been a cornerstone of the parent-child relationship, is shed and replaced by a need for friendship, guidance, and a new level of understanding on the part of the teenager's parents.

An individual entering the teenage years is rapidly developing into an adult and becoming increasingly capable of determining his or her own destiny. For parents, the adolescent years can be a time of witnessing the fruition of the solid groundwork they had laid throughout the childhood years. In it parents can fully enjoy the daily miracle of growth from childhood to adulthood. Much of the pain and pleasure that parents experience with their teenagers during these years is based as much on their perception of the meaning of adolescent behavior as it is on the foundation they have provided for their child throughout his life. In this complex period of transformation, parents *can* be threatened and disoriented, or they can become genuine partners in growth with their teenagers.

How willingly and successfully a parent deals with the inevitable adolescent years is intimately related to his or her own experiences as a youth and belief in the basic goodness of all children. In whatever measure we succeed or fail as parents, we each bring our personal history and principles into the complex process of parenting, and we invariably pass these on to our children, for better or worse. It is during the difficult years of adolescence that we are first able to judge our own successes and failures, as well as make the personal changes necessary to help our children in the most meaningful ways.

Teenagers face enormous difficulties and challenges, in every corner of our society. We live in a country that is fraught with dangers and violence; it is also ripe with opportunities and distractions. Everything our children confront in their day-to-day lives is on a grander scale than we experienced as children, and much of what they encounter is new and dangerous. Today's adolescents must cope with such difficult and life-threatening issues as HIV/AIDS, gang violence, pervasive drug use, and enormous societal pressures that we, as parents, were generally spared. It is a hard job growing up in contemporary America, and it is even more difficult to do so successfully. The rules of the adolescent game are more complex now than they were when we were teenagers, and we must be quick to recognize that our children need all the help and support we can provide.

However, despite the obvious difficulties faced by adolescents and their parents, we each have a powerful tool at our disposal—love. There is a natural and special bond between parents and their children, which is usually incredibly strong and resilient. Although it is true that there are many families in this country where love has been eroded, perverted, or destroyed, these are the exception and not the rule. Moreover, it is not our children who destroy love in a family; rather, they can enhance it and give it new meaning. As parents, *we* are responsible for family love—we are the ones who can cultivate it and help it blossom, or destroy it. If we let love slip away from the family environment, we are endangering our children, their children, and the future of our society.

Even in a family where love is plentiful, obvious, and unquestioned, parents must also lead the way into adulthood for their teenagers. This can be a daunting and frightening responsibility. However, meeting this responsibility can also become the basis for an enduring sense of pride as well as the fountainhead of a new phase in the parent-child relationship that can last a lifetime. Our children expect us to guide them successfully into adulthood, even though they rarely express this need (or often seem to reject it entirely). As parents, we must embrace this responsibility and see it through to the end, even though it means years replete with inevitable moments of surprise and pain as well as pleasure.

Volumes have been written about how best to guide our children through their adolescent years. Opinions on this subject are as plentiful as our children. In the final analysis, our successes and failures in parenting become most obvious when our children embark on their own path to parenthood. Only then can we reach some final conclusion as to our own success as parents. Given love, patience, understanding, and persistence, we will find that we have done our job well and can reap the inestimable rewards that come with the unique relationship between parents and their adult children.

In the meantime, while we are in the throes of raising a teenager, *we* need as much support and help as we can get. Like our rapidly growing and changing teenager, we must have direction in our decisions because they are so critical to our ultimate success or failure. If we are raising our first teenager, we will share a unique bond with our child—we will find ourselves in a new and complex period in life that must be seized in a true partnership with our son or daughter. Like our teenager, we will be thrown into a new phase of personal development that can be trying, painful, wonderful, and exciting. Regardless of the number of unexpected changes that we have experienced along with our child in his or her teenage years, we must be ready for anything in the future. To prepare ourselves in the best possible way to succeed in our role as parents, we must identify some basic guidelines to help keep us on track and moving ahead in meeting our enormous responsibilities. As a family, we must have ground rules that are understood, appreciated, and practical. Here are just a few of the most essential:

Be a Great Communicator. Parents are often shocked and saddened when their child enters his or her adolescent years and suddenly stops communicating with them. Overnight, the talkative, cuddly, responsive child of yesterday seems to have been transformed into the reticent, withdrawn teenager of today. In many cases, this change can be profound and troubling to all other family members.

From the parents' point of view, subjects that were once freely discussed have suddenly and mysteriously disappeared from casual conversation. Parents' legitimate questions are now viewed with disdain and distrust or are seen by the teenager as an intrusion into a secret world that appears to him or her utterly beyond adult understanding. In a moment of anguish, parents frequently discover that they really do not know very much about their son or daughter. The simple, open behavior of childhood has been replaced with thick, onion-skin layers of vagaries and amorphous bits of information that seem designed to keep the most concerned, loving parents at bay. In many cases parents are hurt and angered at this abrupt, seemingly unwarranted change in their children. Sadly, if this is their reaction, they may be doing something that can only make matters worse, effectively withdrawing from their teenager.

The reasons why a teenager begins to withdraw from his or her former ways of communicating with parents are not gener-ally nefarious or, in fact, unusual. Among other things, adoles-cence marks the beginning of a separation phase between a child and his or her parents, the initiation of a new relationship that is fundamental to a teenager's successful entry into adult-hood. From the parents' point of view, the first casualty of this transition may be what had always seemed good parent-child communication. However, in reality, communication has not collapsed; rather, the rules of the game have changed—at least from the teenager's perspective.

For the parent, this new phase in the relationship de-mands expert communication abilities. Many parents inher-ently sense this change in the communication ground rules and are able to adjust the ways they approach their child, while others are put off by what seems to be a near-instantaneous and baseless upheaval in behavior. Despite the temptation to be hurt, angry, and withdrawn, it is vital that parents redouble their efforts to keep lines of communication open. Often this requires a good deal of imagination and tenacity.

It is important to understand that teenagers *do* communi-cate: they just do it in ways that are very different than those of children. The openness and vulnerability of childhood is not the way of an adolescent, and this is as it should be. Teenagers are actively working out their roles in the family, among their friends and classmates, and in society. Often they are subtly communicating new understandings about themselves and searching for a genuine understanding of those around them, including family members. This is a time when the adolescent questions everything, including all that has been passed on from his or her parents. It is not an easy time for many parents, nor is it comfortable for their children. However, it is a necessary and important growth process.

Great communicators are able to transcend the differences between parties. They are capable of putting aside their personal preferences and prejudices for the sake of reaching an understanding. For a parent this is a tall task, because it may sometimes seem certain that their teenager is heading down the wrong path in life. However, teenagers, like most of us, are not fond of an unreasonably tight leash. Successful communication with a teenager demands persuasion, patience, a willingness to withhold judgement until all sides have been heard, and, most important, complete honesty. Anything short of this high standard will become immediately apparent to the ever-vigilant adolescent, and he or she will form an instant opinion about the sincerity of the speaker that may not be in anyone's best interest.

Be a Great Listener. It is tempting to engage in "half-listening" when interacting with a teenager. As parents, we have become accustomed to listening to the rapid-fire, sometimes nonsensical gabbing of our children as they grow. Not carefully listening to a younger child seems to be a harmless oversight in most situations. However, the inane babble of a six-year-old has little in common with what a sixteen-year-old has to say. We can probably get away with half-listening to a six-year-old; however, as parents, we had better give full and obvious attention to our teenagers if we want to have any chance of effectively communicating with them. From an adolescent's perspective, they are communicating concepts and beliefs that are often crucial. If their words fall on apparently deaf ears, a teenager can quickly assume that an apparently uninterested parent is an uncaring one.

Recapture Your Memories of Adolescence and Open Your Mind. It is human nature to see everything and everyone from a highly personal point of view. This is not inherently a bad thing, but it can be limiting. As adults, our memories of adolescence are not vivid. Moreover, they are often not accurate. Certainly, for most of us the raw, emotional edge of adolescence has been dulled and leveled over time. Because we are human, and because we are older, we view the critical events of adolescence with less intense emotional involvement and a broader perspective than our children. We are, after all, a generation apart.

However, even as aging adults we *can* recapture the essence of the memories of our own teenage years and use this information to help our children. Within these misplaced memories lie the same experiences that our children encounter in their adolescence. We too were driven by a cornucopia of new emotions, unfamiliar experiences, and overpowering feelings as we entered our teenage years. We too strove to assert ourselves among those around us and to find our own path in our own way. Like our teenage children, we began the process of reevaluating relationships that marked the beginning of our transition to adulthood. All of those teenage experiences that now seem unfamiliar and uncomfortable to us as adults were once the unquestioned companions of our own adolescence.

When we communicate with our teenage children, we must do so against the true backdrop of our own recollections of adolescence, not against the idealized version that we may prefer to remember. It is not enough for us to listen and communicate with our sons and daughters; we must do so with an understanding of their perspectives and experiences. Fortunately, nature has given us a way to do so—memory. If we turn once again to those lost memories, bringing them forward with honesty and complete with the feelings we experienced as adolescents, our efforts to understand our children will be more productive and meaningful.

Be a Great Example. Teenagers may often seem uninterested in their family environment, but they are not. In fact, teenagers are practiced and sophisticated observers of what goes on around them, particularly in the home and with their parents. Beyond that, an adolescent retains a strong and current memory of childhood events, both good and bad. What a teenager sees, he or she retains and may often emulate.

There could be no more false, overused, or irrelevant turn of the phrase than "Do what I say, not what I do." In fact, any parent who uses this phrase in earnest is essentially asking their teenager to be dishonest, untrustworthy, and hypocritical. As parents, every action we take is subject to observation, analysis, and emulation by our teenage sons and daughters. In truth, it often matters very little what we say, but what we do is enormously important. The worst scenario we can create for our teenager is one of dishonesty and hypocrisy. If we kill trust in the relationship with our sons or daughters, we have doomed the relationship.

Not only must we set the highest example of honesty and trust, we must be quick to recognize our own failures and forgive them, as we would with any loved one. A teenager will judge us more by our history and actions than by our words or intent. Therefore, we must be clear and open in what we do. We must also be willing to openly and honestly correct our own mistakes, put pride in its proper place, and show a ready sense of forgiveness. If we merely give lip service to these ideals, our teenagers will follow in our misguided path.

Be Involved but Not Overbearing. Like any human being, a teenager craves nurturing and understanding. However, too much of a good thing can spoil the meal. Teenagers are in a constant struggle for their independence—a struggle that is often difficult and confusing. Like any of us who are under a good deal of pressure in our lives, our adolescent sons and daughters need a place where they are appropriately loved, understood, and accepted. They do not need a place where they are unduly inspected, unreasonably questioned, and habitually distrusted.

The successful parent of a teenager is a master at balancing the emotional forces in a family environment. Instinctively, successful parents know when to approach their teenager to offer help and advice and when to withdraw with an assurance that they will always be there, day or night, under any circumstances. Teenagers want their parents to be involved in their lives, but only on *their* terms; parents want to be involved with their children, but on *their* terms. Somewhere in the middle of this spectrum of involvement lies success and effective communication.

The way to find the most effective level of involvement in a teenager's life is to talk about it. The sure way to miss the mark and destroy open communications with a son or daughter is to be over-involved or under-involved. In either its excess or its absence, involvement is a delicate issue with adolescents, a subject that is perennially open for negotiation, renegotiation, and changes in tactics based on understanding and love. In whatever level it takes, the correct balance of involvement has been accomplished when the parents are comfortable with their knowledge and understanding of their teenager and he or she is comfortable with what they know.

Setting Limits—Know When to Hold Them, Know When to Fold Them. One of the most frustrating aspects of parenting a teenager can be setting appropriate limits on behavior. However, it is also among the most important of so many parental responsibilities. Throughout the childhood years, parents become accustomed to a sense of complete authority over their children. Suddenly, with the approach of adolescence, this inviolable rule becomes the target of questioning and testing. Many parents do not accept this change well and become frustrated, angry or hurt. However, this period of testing limits and pushing the boundaries of acceptable behavior is natural and necessary for the teenager. It was the same for us when we were young; why should it be different for our children?

At times—perhaps much of the time—parents may feel that they are at war with their teenager over issues of limits. It is natural for a parent to feel this way. If in fact one views this as a war over setting limits, then it is important to remember that it is not necessary to win every battle with a teenager— only the war itself. There is a purpose for testing limits and pushing the boundaries of behavior. It is a learning process for our children and for us.

As parents, we have a responsibility to lead our children into adulthood in a way that is safe, sane, honest, nonviolent, productive, and provides them with the best opportunities for success. These are some of the important criteria by which we set limits on our own behavior, and there is no reason why these same ideals should not apply to our teenagers. The key to using these criteria in setting behavioral limits is to make sure that our sons and daughters not only understand each one but they also understand *why* we feel they are valuable and inviolable. Perhaps the most common mistake made by parents in trying to set limits on behavior is failure to explain the purpose or basis for their actions, except in the most general terms. We cannot expect our bright, inquisitive, and sponge-like sons and daughters merely to accept our demands for different behavior with nothing more than a vague reference to the good of the concept. We may want them to follow our lead simply because we offer it; however, if we act in this way we are not recognizing the importance of adolescence itself as a learning time. We are also failing to understand the relationship reevaluation process that is going on with our child.

Setting limits is vital to the developmental success of teenagers. It is also desired by our sons and daughters, although this desire may often not be apparent. Adolescents want to understand the entire world around them, and few things are more important to them than family and friends. However, like the rest of us, they also want to understand the *reasons* for things—especially when the rules conflict with their desires. Therefore, the best course of action is to negotiate rules of behavior so that there is no misunderstanding, always with the underlying commitment to the fundamental principles that make for a successful adult life.

Be a Good Friend. When our children reach their teenage years, it is a very short journey to adulthood and a world apart from childhood. It may be painful to admit, but in some ways parents become less important in the adolescent years, while meaningful and trusted friendships become critical. Teenagers are adults waiting to happen, not children waiting passively to be led. It is during this phase of their growth that friends take on a new and transforming role in the lives of our sons and daughters. Fortunately, as parents we can become our teenager's close friends—perhaps even his or her best friends—if we are ready and willing to take on this new, important role while we carefully shed our old relationship.

To be successful as parents, we must forge a true partnership with our adolescent sons and daughters. This partnership must be based on honesty, a mutual understanding of the roles of the partners, respect, and trust. These are the building blocks of a friendship that can last a lifetime and make an enormous difference in how we meet our responsibilities as parents.

Be Observant. Most experts in adolescent psychology agree that teenagers often show warning signs of impending emotional difficulties, including potential violence. Significant changes in behavior, personal habits, sleeping patterns, deteriorating performance at school or other activities, or withdrawal from friends and family can indicate that a teenager is undergoing important and troublesome life experiences. Most significant are abrupt changes in relationships that indicate the adolescent is becoming unusually withdrawn from his or her peers. One clue to this potential problem is the absence of a close friend. It is normal for a teenager to have at least one very close and trusted friend. If an adolescent suddenly has no close friends, this is a warning sign that should not be ignored. At these times of crucial change, it is imperative that a teenager's parents remain close and supportive, but not overly intrusive and overbearing. It is essential that parents communicate openly and in an understanding way with their teenager, to work mutually toward a level of trust and understanding that can help their child through the inevitable turbulence of growing up. This same level of alertness to emotional issues should be exercised by other adults who come into regular contact with our teenagers, such as school counselors and teachers.

Show Your Love. Say it, demonstrate it, prove it, and always mean it. An adolescent may be reticent to show the love and affection of a child, but he or she is very acutely attuned to even the most subtle clues of acceptance or rejection. It is not enough to rely on the assumption that love is present in a parent-teenager relationship. It is vital that the teenager know and experience the kind of parental love that is appropriate to his or her changing and challenging life. Of all the things we can do for our children as they grow, the most important is to teach them the meaning and beauty of genuine love.

A FUTURE FOR OUR CHILDREN

There is no question that we are living in an increasingly dangerous and aggressive society. Despite the fact that America has recently experienced a modest decrease in major crime, our society has grown progressively more violent for several decades. Moreover, there is reason to believe that this disturbing trend will continue into the next century, particularly among the tens of millions of children who will enter their teenage years over the next decade or two.

Not only have our lives been directly affected by an increasingly violent society, but the lives of our teenage sons and daughters are also more at risk today than ever before in our nation's history. Our children live in a decidedly menacing and volatile world, beset by challenges and obstacles that did not exist or were insignificant when we were their age. For example, Table 7.1 outlines the most pressing disciplinary problems faced by high school teachers in 1940 and 1990 in dealing with their pupils. The cultural changes implied by this data are astounding.

Table 7.1
Top Disciplinary Problems Identified by High School Teachers (1940 and 1990)

1940	1990
Talking out of turn	Drug abuse
Chewing gum	Alcohol abuse
Making noise	Pregnancy
Running in the hall	Suicide
Cutting in line	Rape
Dress code violations	Robbery
Littering	Assault

Source: American Psychological Association, "All That Violence Is Numbing," undated monograph, (Internet Edition), citing statistics first appearing in *U.S. News and World Report*, 1992.

Whereas the high school social environment of 1940 was compromised only by what we recognize today as minor behavioral problems, our teenagers now must confront very real issues of life and death on a daily basis. In fact, the majority of pressing disciplinary problems identified by high school teachers in 1990 are felonious violations of the law, not merely the disruptive behavior that seemed so worrisome in 1940. It is obvious that the social problems that we encountered throughout our adolescence are not nearly as significant as those faced by our teenage sons and daughters. Minor behavioral issues have been pushed far to the background and replaced by such overwhelming social challenges as drugs, violent crime, pregnancy, and suicide. These are challenges of such a magnitude that our children cannot be expected to pass through their adolescence without significant personal risk and a pressing need for better information, more meaningful support, and a greater level of common sense than was ever expected in our time.

At the same time that our children must confront so many overwhelming social issues, we as parents seem to have become less effective in guiding them through the hazardous adolescent years. It seems that many parents have simply not kept pace with the increasing challenges in their own lives and the new, ominous risks to the lives of their children. It is not that today's parents love their children less, but that the job of parenting has become an awesome, complex responsibility, which has been made even more difficult by the inherent and growing dangers in American society.

Our country has witnessed a persistent erosion of the strength of the family unit for several decades. Today there are more divorces, more broken families, more domestic violence, and more single-parent households than ever before in our history. However, we continue to produce children at a rapid pace. Certainly, these two critical dynamics of our contemporary culture are on a collision course, and they will not slip silently away without a profound impact on us all.

The enormous benefits of a stable family in which at least one parent has a good deal of time to spend with his or her children is a thing of the past. Today, many children are raised in single-parent households that border on poverty and in which the parent must struggle to work as well as be a guardian and mentor to the children. Even in two-parent households, it is common to find that both adults must work to support the basic needs of the family. Just as in a single-parent household, working partners do not have as much time to spend with their children as did parents of past generations. The unintentional withdrawal of abundant parental presence and support comes at a time when our children need it most in order to maximize their abilities to avoid the many opportunities for disaster that they will inevitably face. Surely, this is not a happy confluence of circumstances for any American, of any age.

Even in affluent families, the presence of two parents in the household who are able to spend a generous amount of time with their children is not nearly as common as it once was. In many ways and for many reasons, the contemporary lifestyle of the average American is more complex and fast-paced, less centered on the family unit, than it has ever been. In so many ways, we seem to be a generation of parents that has moved inexorably and unwillingly away from our children in their greatest time of need. Now, we are confronted with the results of our absence in their lives, which is all too often shocking aggression, violence, and self-destructive behavior.

Even in what one might consider to be an ideal family environment, where there is sufficient time to spend with the children, many parents have withdrawn from modes of mentoring that are crucial to a child's development. Many parents have distanced themselves from the traditional practice of passing on valued mores to their children within the family environment. In previous generations the family was a learning environment as well as a nurturing one; today we may still maintain a nurturing family environment, but we have gradually and unknowingly withdrawn from our equally important roles as teachers and mentors for our children. Increasingly, we now look to institutions and organizations outside the family to provide education and example setting for our children. Clearly, this expectation closes the door to the important tradition of personally mentoring our children through example, explanation, and discussion of crucial social and moral values.

As a society, we have come to doubt and fear our own children. For many adults, adolescents are individuals to be avoided because they represent risk. This is an understandable reaction to the increasing levels of violence among our children; however, this fear and withdrawal compounds the already complex and tenuous relationships that exist naturally between generations. In many ways we do not understand our teenage sons and daughters, and this lack of understanding can lead to distrust and fear if it is not overcome by reaching out to our children in a positive, tolerant, and loving way.

As parents we often forget that our parents, too, viewed us with skepticism and doubt. We too were seen as rebellious, misguided, and without direction. However, the challenges of our generation were relatively simple in comparison to those faced by our children. When our own teenagers go wrong, they can go horribly wrong, and as adults we understand and dread this possibility. If as teenagers we grew our hair too long, dressed in what was perceived as an absurd way, or flaunted the advice of our parents, there was little inherent threat to society in our actions; today, however, the issues that we associate with adolescents are guns, random violence, lethal gangs, and unprecedented acts of aggression. It is this kind of criminal behavior that we fear and this kind of violence that we seem unable to control. Because of this fear we unintentionally withdraw from teenage members of our society, and in so doing we push them even farther from the sources of love and guidance that they most need.

Today there are more than forty million children under the age of ten living in America. They will soon enter their teenage years; many of these children are already beginning to face the overwhelming challenges that are a fundamental part of our complex, sometimes chaotic, society. Most of these children are good kids and will remain so throughout their adolescent years. However, many—far too many—will become the victims of our complex, aggressive society—victims who, in turn, may become predators. These are the children we will fear the most, and they are also the ones who need our help and support *now*.

Some of tomorrow's teenagers will shock us with crimes of violence that seem beyond any reason or purpose. They will be known as good kids who kill, unless we as parents throw ourselves into a commitment without compromise to ensure that this does not happen. Our children want and deserve a life free from fear and violence, just as we do, and they rightfully look to us to do what we can to ensure their future. For their sake and ours, we cannot ignore them or assume that some-one else will help them face the overwhelming challenges of adolescence.

NOTES

1. Emily Benedek, "A Death in the Family," *Redbook* (Inter-net Edition), 1 August 1994.

2. Allan Abrahamse, "The Coming Wave of Violence in Cali-fornia," RAND Corporation Documented Briefing, 1997, 11.

3. Ibid.

4. Louise Farr, "When Young Passion Kills," *Redbook* (Inter-net Edition), 1 October 1994.

About the Author

MICHAEL D. KELLEHER, who has written widely on the subject of violence, specializes in threat assessment, strategic management, and human resources management for organizations in the private and public sectors. He is the author of *Murder Most Rare*, *Profiling the Lethal Employee*, *Flash Point: The American Mass Murderer*, and *New Arenas for Violence* (1996), all published by Praeger.

APPENDIX

I. FACT, FICTION, AND JUVENILE VIOLENCE

How much do we really know about our teenage sons and daughters? What is the reality of teenage violence and crime, and what is fiction? Here is a random collection of facts that may be surprising to many:

- There are currently more than forty million children under the age of ten in America, who will enter their teenage years at the beginning of the new millennium.
- If the current juvenile arrest rate remains constant, some experts predict a 22 to 30 percent hike in the number of juveniles who will be charged with crimes in the year 2010. However, if the annual number of juvenile arrests continues to increase at the rate experienced over the past seven years, this number will approximately double by that year.
- Approximately 25 percent of our children now live in poverty, giving our country the dubious distinction of one of the highest poverty rates for children among all economically advantaged nations.
- More than 25 percent of our children live with only one parent.
- Teenagers currently commit more than four thousand murders

each year, and some experts believe that this number will grow to at least five thousand by the year 2010.

- The problem of juvenile violence is not limited to the United States; in fact, it plagues other countries to a great extent. In Russia, an adolescent is involved in one out of every ten crimes. However, in many countries, like Canada, the general surge in adolescent crime has not matched that of the United States.

- By the age of eighteen the average adolescent will have viewed an estimated 200,000 acts of violence on television. This does not include exposure to other forms of violence, such as at the cinema, media entertainment, or some sporting events.

- According to the Federal Bureau of Investigation *Uniform Crime Report* for 1995, over 677,000 arrests were made for crimes committed by individuals under the age of eighteen that year. Of these, over 115,000 arrests were for violent crimes.

- The risk that a teenager will die by a firearm more than doubled in the ten years between 1985 and 1994. In 1995, 8 percent of American high school students *admitted* to carrying a firearm routinely for fighting or self-defense.

- In 1995, the Justice Department reported that 83 percent of incarcerated juveniles claimed that they owned a gun, and 35 percent of them stated that it was acceptable to use that weapon to injure or kill another person.

- The Centers for Disease Control (CDC) reported in February 1997 that 2.57 out of every hundred thousand Americans under the age of fifteen were killed by a firearm, as compared to an average rate of 0.51 per hundred thousand in twenty-five other countries surveyed.

- The number of juveniles who were confirmed victims of homicide tripled in the ten years between 1984 and 1994.

- The American Civil Liberties Union (ACLU) reported in mid-1996 that some states, such as California and Florida, spend more on juvenile corrections than they spend on higher education. They reported the average cost of incarcerating a juvenile for one year as between $35,000 and $64,000, while important programs such as Head Start spent only $4,300 annually on each enrolled child. By comparison, the annual tuition cost of attending Harvard University was less than the minimum expenditure per offender on corrections ($30,000) in the same year surveyed.

• Juvenile gang-related murders increased approximately 400 percent between 1980 and 1992. By 1994, the United States Justice Department has reported an average of seven juveniles per day were victims of homicide, many at the hands of gang members.

• The number of Americans, including adolescents, now incarcerated in jails and prisons has doubled in the past decade and currently surpasses a million persons.

• A 1994 Gallup poll reported that the average American adult believed that adolescents commit 43 percent of all violent crimes in the United States. However, in that year, they were actually responsible for only 13 percent of such crimes.

• Parents are six times more likely to murder their children than children are likely to murder their parents.

II. SELECTED REFERENCE READING: CHILDHOOD EXPERIENCES AND DELINQUENCY

This is a selection of scholarly references that examine the impact of negative or abusive childhood experiences on later violent adolescent behavior.

Bowers, Laurene B. "Traumas Precipitating Female Delinquency: Implications for Assessment, Practice, and Policy." *Child and Adolescent Social Work Journal* 7 (5), 389–402 (October 1990).

Brown, Stephen E. "Social Class, Child Maltreatment, and Delinquent Behavior." *Criminology: An Interdisciplinary Journal* 22 (2), 259–278 (May 1984).

Gray, Ellen. "The Link between Child Abuse and Juvenile Delinquency: What We Know and Recommendations for Policy and Research." In Gerald T. Hotaling et al., eds., *Family Abuse and Its Consequences: New Directions in Research*. Newbury Park, CA: Sage, 1988, 109–123.

Rivera, B., and C. S. Windom. "Childhood Victimization and Violent Offending." *Violence and Victims* (1996), 5, 19–25.

Windom, C. S. "Victims of Childhood Sexual Abuse: Later Criminal Consequences." National Institute of Justice *Research in Brief* (March 1995), 1–8.

III. SELECTED REFERENCE READING: NEONATICIDE

These references examine the issue of neonaticide committed by women, particularly young mothers.

Bonnet, C. "Adoption at Birth: Prevention against Abandonment or Neonaticide." *Child Abuse and Neglect* 17 (4), 501–513 (1993).

Goetting, A. "Child Victims of Homicide: A Portrait of Their Killers and the Circumstances of Their Deaths." *Violence and Victims* 5 (4), 287–296 (1991).

Unnithan, N. P. "Children As Victims of Homicide: Making Claims, Formulating Categories, and Constructing Social Problems." *Deviant Behavior* 15 (1), 63–83 (1994).

Van Biema, D. "Parents Who Kill." *Time,* 14 November 1994, 50–51.

Williamson, G. L. "Postpartum Depression Syndrome As a Defense to Criminal Behavior." *Journal of Family Violence* 8 (2), 151–165 (1993).

IV. A SELECTION OF INTERNET SITES: VIOLENT JUVENILE CRIME

There are many Internet sites that present information about juvenile delinquency, the juvenile justice system, and violent juvenile crime. This is a short selection of some of the Internet sites that have made valuable information freely available to the public. These sites express widely divergent views on the subject. However, they each provide valuable information about the difficult subject of violence among our children.

Table A1
Internet Sites with Information on Juvenile Crime

Internet Site	Internet Address (URL)
Justice Information Center (National Criminal Justice Reference Service)	http://www.ncjrs.org
Crime-Free America	http://crime-free.org
The United States Senate	http://www.senate.gov
American Civil Liberties Union	http://www.aclu.org
United States Department of Justice	http://www.ojp.usdoj.gov
American Psychological Association	http://www.apa.org
National Center for Policy Analysis	http://www.ncpa.org
PBS Online	http://www.pbs.org
Florida State University	http://www.fsu.edu
Juvenile Crime and Justice Research in Kansas	http://www.kanzafoundation.org
University of Wisconsin-Milwaukee	http://www.uwm.edu
Vera Institute of Justice	http://broadway.vera.org
The Institute for Intergovernmental Research	http://www.iir.com
The RAND Corporation	http://www.rand.org

SELECTED BIBLIOGRAPHY

Abagnale, F. W., Jr. *Catch Me If You Can*. New York: Pocket Books, 1980.

Abrahamse, Allan. "The Coming Wave of Violence in California." RAND Corporation Documented Briefing, Santa Monica, CA: RAND Corporation, 1997.

Abrahamsen, D. *The Murdering Mind*. New York: Harper Colophon, 1984.

American Psychiatric Association (APA). *Diagnostic and Statistical Manual of Mental Disorders (DSM IV)*. 4th edition. Washington, DC: APA, 1994.

Annie E. Casey Foundation. *Kids Count Data Book: State Profiles of Child Well-being*. Baltimore: Annie E. Casey Foundation, 1993.

Cohn, A. H. *It Shouldn't Hurt to Be a Child*. Chicago: The National Committee for the Prevention of Child Abuse, 1986.

Collins, Huntly. "Friends and Family Can Spot the Signs a Teenager Needs Help." *Philadelphia Inquirer* (Internet Edition), 3 October 1997.

Court Television (CTV). *Massachusetts v. O'Brien—Court TV Library* (Internet Edition). New York: CTV, 1997.

Crespi, Tony D., and Sandra A. Rigazio-DiGillo. "Adolescent Homicide and Family Pathology: Implications for Research and Treatment with Adolescents." *Adolescence* (Internet Edition), 1 June 1996.

Daly, M., and M. Wilson. *Homicide.* New York: Aldine Degruyter, 1988.

Eitzen, D. S., and D. A. Timmer. *Criminology.* New York: Wiley, 1985.

Ewing, Charles Patrick. *Kids Who Kill.* New York: Avon Books, 1992.

Fox, J. A., and J. Levin. *Mass Murder: America's Growing Menace.* New York: Plenum, 1985.

———. *Overkill: Mass Murder and Serial Killing Exposed.* New York: Plenum, 1994.

Garbarino, J., and W. Groninger. *Child Abuse, Delinquency, and Crime.* Chicago: The National Committee for the Prevention of Child Abuse, 1983.

Gaute, J. H. *Murderers Who's Who.* New York: Methuen, 1979.

Goldman, H. H., ed. *Review of General Psychiatry.* Norwalk, CT: Appleton and Lange, 1988.

Heubusch, Kevin. "Teens on the Trigger." *American Demographics* (Internet Edition), February 1997.

Holhut, Randolph T. *Teen Violence: The Myths and the Realities.* Privately published on the Internet, 1996.

Holmes, Ronald M. *Profiling Violent Crimes: An Investigative Tool.* Newbury Park, CA: Sage, 1990.

Holmes, Ronald M., and S. T. Holmes. *Murder in America.* Thousand Oaks, CA: Sage, 1994.

Jones, Michael A., and Barry Krisberg. *Images and Reality: Juvenile Crime, Youth Violence, and Public Policy.* San Francisco: National Council on Crime and Delinquency, 1994.

Klein, Matthew. "Kids and Guns: All-American." *American Demographics* (Internet Edition), 1 July 1997.

Lester, David. *Questions and Answers about Murder.* Philadelphia: Charles Press, 1991.

Magid, Ken, and Carole A. McKelvey. *High Risk: Children without a Conscience.* New York: Bantam, 1987.

Males, Mike, and Faye Docuyanan. "Giving Up on the Young." *The Progressive,* 1 February 1996.

Megargee, E. I., and M. J. Bohn. *Classifying Criminal Offenders.* Newbury Park, CA: Sage, 1979.

Microsoft. *Encarta 96 Encyclopedia* (MS-Windows 95). Redmond, WA: Microsoft, 1996.

———. *Microsoft Bookshelf* (MS-Windows 95). Redmond, WA: Microsoft, 1995.

Moore, Kristin A., et al. *Beginning Too Soon: Adolescent Sexual Behavior, Pregnancy, and Parenthood.* Washington, DC: Child Trends, Inc., 1995.

Office of Juvenile Justice and Delinquency Prevention (OJJDP). *Juvenile Offenders and Victims: 1996 Update on Violence.* Washington, DC: Department of Justice, 1996.

Ressler, Robert K., Ann W. Burgess, and John E. Douglas. *Sexual Homicide: Patterns and Motives.* New York: Lexington, 1988.

Sifakis, C. *The Encyclopedia of American Crime.* New York: Facts on File, 1982.

Snyder, Howard N., and Terrence A. Finnegan. *Easy Access to the FBI's Supplementary Homicide Reports: 1980–1995.* Washington, DC: Office of Juvenile Justice and Delinquency Prevention, 1997.

United States Federal Bureau of Investigation. *Uniform Crime Report: 1995.* Washington, DC: Federal Bureau of Investigation, 1996.

Wilson, Colin, and Damon Wilson. *The Killers among Us.* New York: Time Warner, 1996.

Wolfgang, M., and F. Ferracuti. *The Subculture of Violence.* New York: Tavistock, 1969.

INDEX